HEURISTICS AND HYPER-HEURISTICS - PRINCIPLES AND APPLICATIONS

Edited by **Javier Del Ser Lorente**

Heuristics and Hyper-Heuristics - Principles and Applications
http://dx.doi.org/10.5772/66267
Edited by Javier Del Ser Lorente

Contributors

Satyasundara Mahapatra, Rati Ranjan Dash, Sateesh Kumar Pradhan, Mashael Maashi, Marcos Seruffo, Adamo Lima De Santana, Nadamundi Vijaykumar, Carlos Renato Francês, Nodari Vakhania, Aleksandra Swiercz, Boaz Benmoshe, Roi Yozevitch

Published by InTech

Janeza Trdine 9, 51000 Rijeka, Croatia

Publishing Process Manager Mirena Calmic
Technical Editor SPi Global
Cover InTech Design team

First published August, 2017
Printed in Croatia
Legal deposit, Croatia: National and University Library in Zagreb

Additional hard copies can be obtained from orders@intechopen.com

Heuristics and Hyper-Heuristics - Principles and Applications, Edited by Javier Del Ser Lorente
p. cm.
Print ISBN 978-953-51-3383-4
Online ISBN 978-953-51-3384-1

For EU product safety concerns:
IN TECH d.o.o., Prolaz Marije Krucifikse Kozulić 3, 51000 Rijeka, Croatia,
info@intechopen.com or visit our website at intechopen.com.

Meet the editor

Javier Del Ser received his first PhD degree in Telecommunication Engineering (cum laude) from the University of Navarra, Spain, in 2006, and a second PhD degree in Computational Intelligence (summa cum laude) from the University of Alcala, Spain, in 2013. He is currently a principal researcher in data analytics and optimization at TECNALIA (Spain), a visiting fellow at the Basque Center for Applied Mathematics and an adjunct professor at the University of the Basque Country (UPV/EHU). His research activity gravitates on the use of descriptive, prescriptive and predictive algorithms for data mining and optimization in a diverse range of application fields such as energy, transport, telecommunications, health and security, among many others. In these fields, he has published more than 160 publications, co-supervised 6 PhD degree theses, edited 3 books, co-authored 6 patents and led more than 35 research projects. Dr. Del Ser is a recipient of the Talent of Bizkaia award for his research career.

Contents

Preface

In the last few years, the society is witnessing ever-growing levels of complexity in the optimization paradigms lying at the core of different applications and processes. Most applications stemming from medicine, industry, transport, energy and many other domains can be formulated as an optimization problem with stringent requirements in terms of timing, constraints and manageability. Unfortunately, in many of such problems, the use of off-the-shelf solvers from convex and linear optimization does not suffice for exploring efficiently the space of possible solutions. This shortcoming motivates the adoption of heuristic methods as a means to balance the Pareto trade-off between computational efficiency and the quality of the produced solutions to the problem at hand. The momentum gained by heuristics in practical applications spans further towards hyper-heuristics, which allow constructing ensembles of simple heuristics to handle efficiently several problems of a single class. In this context, this short book compiles selected applications of heuristics and hyper-heuristics for combinatorial optimization problems, including scheduling and other assorted application scenarios. Readers interested in these topics will grasp in this volume an insight on the utility of this family of algorithms through a set of motivating examples.

Javier Del Ser, PhD
TECNALIA Research & Innovation, Spain
University of the Basque Country (UPV/EHU), Spain
Basque Center for Applied Mathematics (BCAM), Spain

Section 1

Heuristics and Hyper-Heuristics

Chapter 1

Hyper-Heuristics and Metaheuristics for Selected Bio-Inspired Combinatorial Optimization Problems

Aleksandra Swiercz

Additional information is available at the end of the chapter

http://dx.doi.org/10.5772/intechopen.69225

Abstract

Many decision and optimization problems arising in bioinformatics field are time demanding, and several algorithms are designed to solve these problems or to improve their current best solution approach. Modeling and implementing a new heuristic algorithm may be time-consuming but has strong motivations: on the one hand, even a small improvement of the new solution may be worth the long time spent on the construction of a new method; on the other hand, there are problems for which good-enough solutions are acceptable which could be achieved at a much lower computational cost. In the first case, specially designed heuristics or metaheuristics are needed, while the latter hyper-heuristics can be proposed. The paper will describe both approaches in different domain problems.

Keywords: hyper-heuristics, bioinformatics

1. Introduction

Many heuristics and metaheuristics (problem-independent algorithmic framework) have been successfully applied for decision and optimization problems. However, there are difficulties in using the already-existing algorithms for new problems or even for new instances of a similar problem. Typically, one needs a time-consuming phase for parameters tuning. The parameters, are often not well-described and do not allow for solving the problem at a satisfactory level (producing satisfactory solutions). Thus, in many cases, one needs to construct new algorithms to solve particular instances. Recently, there have been attempts to automate the process of designing methods to learn the tuning of the parameters. The basic idea is to develop a method which is general and operates on small moves and learns which moves should be applied at each stage of the solving process.

The term hyper-heuristics was first used by Cowling et al. in 2001 [1] for the sales summit problem and refers to a method which does not use the problem-specific information other than a set of simple knowledge poor heuristics which are easy to implement. Between the set of simple low-level heuristics and high-level heuristics, there exists a domain barrier, which does not allow to pass the information about the problem domain. A high-level hyper-heuristic uses performance indicators when a low-level heuristics is called (indicators are not specific to the problem) in order to decide which heuristics should be chosen at a particular time point in the search space. However, the ideas behind hyper-heuristic are not new to the scientific community, and their roots trace back to 1963 and spanned several areas: computer science, artificial intelligence, and operational research. In 1963, Fisher and Thompson [2] showed that combining scheduling rules, known as dispatching or priority rules, is better when they are combined rather than used separately. In 1990s, the ideas were further explored. Storer et al. [3] designed a few fast problem-specific heuristics and defined neighborhoods within the search space. The approach could be applied with any scheduling objective and was tested for the job shop scheduling problems with the minimum makespan objective. In Fang et al. [4], a genetic algorithm (GA) was developed which tried to avoid difficulties in representing a solution as a chromosome, which is needed by the GA. The proposed method searches abstract regions of the solution space and then uses another method which converts the points generated by the GA into candidate solutions. Drechsler and Becker [5] presented a GA which first, based on benchmark examples, learns a good sequence of basic optimization modules (simple methods) and then applies it to instances of a given problem (computer-aided design of integrated circuits).

Some examples of automated parameter tuning can also be considered as a basis for hyper-heuristics. In Ref. [6], one evolutionary algorithm was used to tune the second one, which solved a particular problem. Also, some approaches of self-adaptation in the parameter tuning of the evolutionary algorithms were summarized in the survey [7].

In the area of machine learning, the idea of choosing the best algorithm for a given problem was first posed by Rice [8]. Following this idea, several projects created specialized systems to help to select/recommend the best method, as for example, Consultant-2 [9] and Teacher (Techniques for the Automated Creation of Heuristics) [10]. Consultant-2 was developed to support the machine learning toolbox. It integrates the knowledge of choosing the proper machine learning algorithms based on the nature of domain data and the domain experts' knowledge of preprocessing and manipulating the data, in order to use the system without directly involving the specialists. On the other hand, Teacher was designed as a system for learning and generalizing heuristics used in problem-solving. Despite the lack of or little domain knowledge, the system was able to improve the existing heuristic methods. The Teacher was successfully applied in the area of process mapping, load balancing, routing, and testing.

The above examples show that the term hyper-heuristics, although did not appear before the year 2000, had circulated in the literature for quite a long time. Since then, the term was used, and the idea further developed in many different problem domains [11, 12].

The methods often used in the context of hyper-heuristics have strong connections with biology. However, the flow of ideas between biology and operational research works in both directions. Observations of nature provide the basis for designing algorithms: many evolutionary and genetic algorithms were used as (hyper-)heuristics to solve combinatorial optimization problems. On the other hand, operational research methods can help solving problems arising in the field of biology and resulted in creating a new area of Bioinformatics. Some examples of problems solved with the use of bioinformatics tools are DNA sequencing, DNA mapping, RNA structure prediction and protein folding. Moreover, mutual infiltration of the ideas of the two scientific domains can work in both directions just for a single problem. The DNA sequencing by hybridization (SBH) problem (further described in Section 4) in the ideal case was first defined as searching for a Hamiltonian path in a special graph [13], which is an NP-hard problem. SBH was later modeled as the search for a Eulerian path that could be solved in polynomial time [14], which is the opposite of searching for a Hamiltonian path problem. Analysis of this phenomenon resulted in defining a new type of DNA graphs and showed why searching for a Hamiltonian and Eulerian path in these two types of graphs is equivalent [15]. For that particular problem, the operational research methods were used to solve the problem, while the analysis of SBH problem introduced a new type of graphs and gave an insight into the connections between easy and NP-hard problems.

The goal of this chapter is to show the connections between the areas of biology, computer science and operational research in the context of (hyper-)heuristics search. Although some surveys on the meta and hyper-heuristic search have been published [11, 12], here we focus mainly on the selected bio-inspired problems solved with hyper-heuristic methods. In the next section, the classification of hyper-heuristic algorithms is presented. Section 3 describes different methods used in the hyper-heuristic framework. The following section focuses on few biological problems successfully solved with hyper-heuristics. In Section 5, we show that not all the problems could be solved with hyper-heuristics and specially tailored-to-measure heuristics are needed. We also propose a small hint how hyper-heuristic search could be incorporated in solving the DNA assembly problem. Section 6 summarizes and highlights a potentially interesting future research direction.

2. Hyper-heuristics and their classification

A hyper-heuristic framework consists of a set of low-level heuristics and a high-level hyper-heuristic algorithm. The latter evaluates the performance of low-level heuristics and selects one of them to change the current solution. The performance can be measured as an increase in the objective function value, defined for the problem, but can also check the time of computations or the time a heuristic was last used. The hyper-heuristic can process one (single point search) or multiple solutions at a time (multi-point search). In the former, an initial candidate solution goes through a set of successive steps until it gets to the final solution. In the latter, utilized for the perturbative methods, a few solutions are processed in parallel, like for example in the AMALGAM approach, which operates on the population of solutions [16]. Apart from the selection of the low-level heuristics, the acceptance mechanism seems to be crucial in the hyper-heuristics research. The decision whether to accept or reject the new solution can be always the same for the same (*deterministic*) or different (*non-deterministic*) input, for example, dependent on the time passed. The process is repeated iteratively, a low-level heuristic is selected from the available ones in the set, the decision is made about the acceptance of the heuristic and in the case of acceptance, it is applied to the solution until a stopping criterion is met. The high-level heuristic has no information about the solved problem and is operating only on the heuristic search space, opposite to metaheuristics which operate on the solution space. The general scheme of the hyper-heuristic framework is presented in **Figure 1**.

In Burke et al. [17], the definition of a hyper-heuristic was further extended to *a search method or selection mechanism for selecting or generating heuristics to solve computational search problems*. The classification of hyper-heuristics presented in surveys [11, 12, 17] takes into account the nature of the heuristic search space and the feedback used for learning mechanism (see **Figure 2**).

According to the nature of the search space, we might have methodologies that *select* existing heuristics to use and methodologies that *generate* new heuristics on the basis of existing smaller components. The second level in this dimension corresponds to the *constructive* and *perturbative* methods. Perturbative methods are using complete candidate solutions and change them by modifying solution components, while constructive methods start from partial candidate solutions and extend them iteratively. This type of approach has been applied to several hard combinatorial problems such as educational timetabling [18–20], production scheduling [21], packing [22] or vehicle routing [23]. In the case of generation methods, hyper-heuristics search the space of heuristics constructed from components rather than well-defined heuristics. The examples where generation hyper-heuristics were used include several domains: timetabling and scheduling [24], the traveling salesman problem [25, 26] or cutting and packing [27–29]. Both classes of hyper-heuristics, selection, and generation, output a solution at the end of a run, but a heuristic generator outputs also new heuristics that produced the solution, and these heuristics could be potentially used for the next problem.

The second dimension corresponds to a learning mechanism which is used by a hyper-heuristic algorithm. If the learning takes place while the algorithm is solving an instance of the problem than we say that there is an *online* feedback. The idea is to learn a good sequence of heuristics for the problems at hand [1, 22, 30].

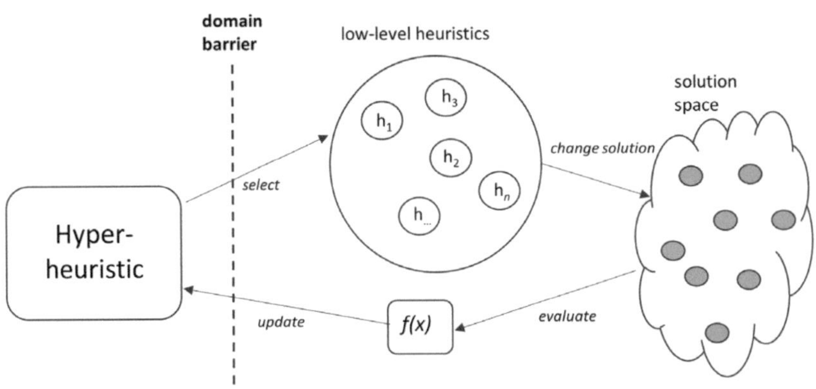

Figure 1. General scheme of how hyper-heuristics work.

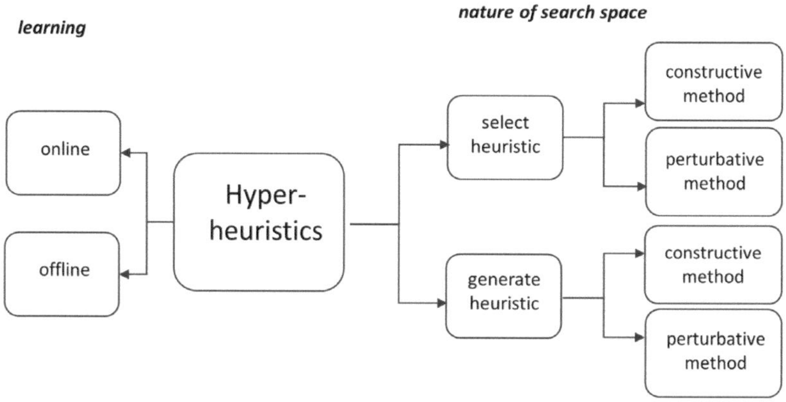

Figure 2. Classification of hyper-heuristics (following Ref. [11]).

In *offline* learning, the idea is to gather knowledge in the form of rules or programs while solving some benchmark instances and hope that these rules are general enough to solve unseen instances [31–33].

There are some methods which do not fit strictly to the frames presented above but rather span across two or more categories. They use either selecting and generating methods [34] or perturbative and constructive heuristics [35].

3. Learning techniques in hyper-heuristics

Learning techniques are key/essential indicators of the quality of hyper-heuristics. Good learning mechanisms impinge on obtaining better solutions and the possibility to reuse the hyper-heuristic and this decrease software production costs. Low-level heuristics are usually simple heuristics designed for a problem, but if used in a wrong order may not allow to get better solutions than when a single such heuristic is applied. Depending on the nature of the search space, different learning mechanisms were used. Below a few of the approaches are mentioned, some of them derived from the observations on biological evolution made by naturalist Charles Darwin. In his concept, the individuals in the population of one species are subject to the natural selection rules to fit the environment better. Among the fitting mechanisms, we can distinguish (i) crossover, reproducing of individuals in order to create a new one(s), (ii) mutation, random change of an individual in order to introduce diversity to the population, and (iii) selection of the best features in the population or in one individual. Biological evolution was an inspiration for developing bio-inspired algorithms like evolutionary algorithms, genetic algorithms or genetic programming. All of them were utilized as hyper-heuristics in different contexts of the nature of the search space. A few examples are mentioned in the following paragraphs.

In the selection mechanism with the combination of constructive heuristics, commonly used local search–based hyper-heuristics explore the solution space with the selected heuristics as widely as possible. A variable neighborhood search was used in the context of examination timetabling [18]. Tabu search-based hyper-heuristic was applied for the workforce scheduling problem [36] and course and exam timetabling [19]. Evolutionary or genetic algorithms were used for solving the vehicle routing problem [35] and bin packing of 2D elements [37].

In case of perturbative low-level heuristics, more commonly used are score-based hyper-heuristics. A choice function was introduced in Ref. [1] which evaluates each heuristic according to a score composed of three components: how well a heuristic performs, how well it performs when combined with another one, and the time elapsed since it was last used. A low-level heuristic can be selected in four different ways (i) *randomly*, (ii) taking the one giving the best value of the choice function (*greedy*), (iii) basing the choice on a *ranking* of best heuristics, or (iv) selecting a heuristic with the probability equal to the proportion of choice function value (*roulette wheel*). Choice function hyper-heuristics solved the sales summit problem [1], timetabling and scheduling [38] and sequencing by hybridization [39]. Reinforcement learning, another score-based approach, awards or punishes heuristics depending on the improvement or deterioration of the solution. It has been applied for the logistic domain problem [40]. In the combination with tabu search, a tabu list of forbidden heuristics was implemented for nurse rostering and course timetabling [41].

The solution obtained by applying a low-level heuristic might not always be improved. There are different strategies in accepting the solution in case of deterioration. 'All accept' always accepts the solution. Some other strategies accept a new solution with the probability that decreases with time: simulated annealing or Monte Carlo.

In generating new heuristics, one usually involves genetic programming (GP). GP, similarly to evolutionary algorithms, borrows ideas from the theory of natural evolution to automatically produce programs [42]. It starts from a population of generated computer programs which are evaluated by the fitness function. Next, evolutionary components (selection, mutation, crossover) are applied to the individuals in the population and the strongest, i.e. the fittest ones, survive in the next generation. The difference between standard GP and the hyper-heuristic GP is in the generality of the programs used. In the standard approach, the programs could be standard arithmetic operations, standard mathematical functions or logical functions, while in the hyper-heuristic approach, the programs are rather abstract heuristics, independent of the problem domain. As the output from the GP, one gets new programs, which in standard approach could be direct solutions (i.e. modified mathematical formulas or arithmetic operations), but in the hyper-heuristic approach, they need to be translated into solutions. Automatically generated heuristics can be *disposable*, used only once, or *reusable*–can be applied for different instances or problems. In the latter case, generating heuristics are usually trained offline on some benchmark instances.

GP hyper-heuristics were utilized to modify dispatching rules for the job shop scheduling problem ([43], as an example). Grammar-based GP with graph coloring and slot allocation heuristics were applied to exam timetabling [24]. Many applications used GP to evolve heuristics also for the bin packing problem [27, 44] and traveling salesmen problem [25, 45].

There is an interesting connection between the idea of reusable heuristics and transfer learning [46]. In both cases, one may observe the transfer of knowledge between different but related problem domains. However, in the first case, hyper-heuristic is used to tune heuristics from one instance to another or to generate new heuristics, and in transfer learning training data of one problem may be used to potentially improve the results of a target learner on a data set from a different domain. Transfer learning is used mostly in cases when there is a lack of training data or they are too expensive to collect.

4. Hyper-heuristics for bio-inspired combinatorial problems

In this section, a few examples are described in more details for which hyper-heuristic methods were used to solve bio-inspired problems. This field has not been explored deeply, and only a few attempts have been made so far. The difficulty here lies in the quality of the solution. For bio-experts, it is often important that the solution is the optimum or very close to the optimum, not just 'good enough'. Moreover, sometimes mathematical models cannot express biological problems well. The optimization function in the model may lead to a few solutions which are mathematically optimal but only one is biologically correct. Three main contributions from the literature are summarized below, one dealing with the longest common subsequence problem and two with the sequencing by hybridization problem.

4.1. Longest common subsequence

The longest Common Subsequence (LCS) problem amounts to find the longest string that is a subsequence of every string in a given set of strings. The subsequence here is not composed of consecutive letters in the string, but it can be achieved by deleting some of the characters from the string. The problem can be solved polynomially in the case of two strings, but in general, the problem is NP-hard. The example of what the LCS problem is explained in **Figure 3**.

The LCS problem is used in bioinformatics to compare sequences of molecules: DNA, RNA or proteins, in order to find homologies between sequences of organisms of different species. The homology helps to predict the function of unknown genes if their sequences are similar to those of known genes one may expect that the function is similar. The other applications of LCS can be found in text editing [47] or data compression [48], among others.

Tabataba and Mousavi [49] proposed a hyper-heuristic for the LCS problem. A beam search algorithm in its standard form is a tree-based procedure. It starts from the initially empty solution and extends it by one letter in every iteration. All possible characters Σ are evaluated by a function *f(.)* as possible extensions, but only β best ones are further explored in the

s_1 = c c a t a g a c c s_2 = a t t t g a t a c

s_3 = g a t g g a a t c s_4 = a g t g a g c t

LCS *solution* = a t g a c

Figure 3. The example of the LCS problem. For a given set of strings *S* = {ccatagacc, atttgatac, gatggaatc, agtgagct}, the longest common subsequence of each string is 'atgac'. The LCS is underlined in every string.

next iteration, β being the size of the beam. A hyper-heuristic approach is introduced here to choose the best function *f(.)* among the two available: *power* and *prob*. *Power* takes into account the length of possible suffixes, with the high impact of the minimum suffix, after deciding on the possible extension character. *Prob*, on the other hand, calculates the probability of a random string being a subsequence of the suffix. The hyper-heuristic runs the beam search algorithm twice in every iteration with *power* and *prob* as *f(.)* function and chooses the one which gives the possibility of a longer subsequence extension.

The method was tested on random biologically inspired and real sequences of DNA and proteins of rats and viruses (Σ equal to 4 in the case of DNA sequences and 20 in the case of proteins). Hyper-heuristic appeared to superior to the beam search method used with just one heuristic, either *power* or *prob*. The proposed hyper-heuristic in comparison with the state-of-art algorithms MLCS-APP and DEA, depending on the tested dataset, provides 1–2% and 19–25% improvements in the solution quality, respectively.

4.2. DNA sequencing by hybridization

Sequencing by hybridization (SBH) is a method used for reading DNA sequences, nowadays not used any more due to high costs, but its concepts can be of value for other real-world applications. It is composed of two phases, biological and computational experiments. The former utilizes a microarray chip to determine all the subsequences of an unknown DNA sequence, i.e. subsequences of a given length k (k-mers). The set of k-mers contained in the DNA sequence is called *spectrum*. The latter, combines the elements from the spectrum, by checking their overlapping, into a longer sequence, that do not exceed the original DNA sequence length, n. The example of an SBH experiment is shown in **Figure 4**.

In the ideal case, the problem is easy, while in the real experiments, two types of errors may occur which make the real problem NP hard. A negative error occurs when a k-mer, being a subsequence of the examined sequence, is missing in the spectrum, while a positive error is an extra element in the spectrum not being a subsequence of the DNA sequence. Note that repeated subsequences in the DNA sequence cause negative errors because they appear only once in the spectrum.

A hyper-heuristic approach was first used to solve the SBH problem in Ref. [39]. The solution is represented as an ordered *list* of elements from the spectrum that contributes to the DNA sequence, and *trash*, an unordered set of 'leftovers' from the spectrum. The sequence is reconstructed with a greedy algorithm that traverses the list and tries to append every k-mer with the smallest shift to the preceding one.

The low-level heuristics operate on the list and trash by moving elements from one set to another. In the basic approach, we can distinguish operations on single elements: insertion from trash to list, deletion from list to trash or shift–moves of the elements within the list; or operations on a cluster–a group of closely connected elements. A cluster can be shifted or deleted. An extended approach changed the encoding of the solution, by allowing elements from the spectrum to appear on the list twice, thus solving the problem of repetitions. Also, several new heuristics were proposed, with *swap* as an example.

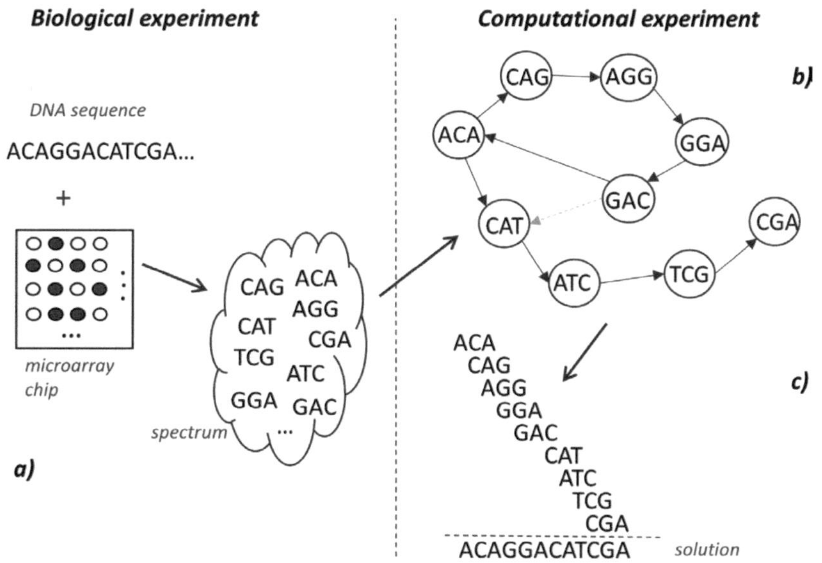

Figure 4. SBH is composed of biological and computational experiments. In the first one (a), a microarray, containing all *k*-mers ($k = 3$), is used to obtain a spectrum. In the latter, elements from the spectrum are modelled as the nodes in the graph in which a Hamiltonian path is looked for (b). Solid arrows represent the overlap of the two nodes equal to 2, and the dashed arrows overlap equal to 1 (most of them are omitted to simplify the picture) meaning that there is a negative error between the two *k*-mers. A path starting from ACA results in obtaining the examined DNA sequence, see the layout in (c). However, notice that starting from node CAG one may obtain a different, shorter solution composed of the same number of elements from the spectrum.

A few hyper-heuristics were proposed, namely a tabu search algorithm, choice function approaches (roulette, ranked, best and decomp), and a simulated annealing algorithm. In the first method, all moves were accepted, while the last method used the Monte Carlo approach which could reject a deteriorated solution with the probability that increased with the passed time. The results of the computational experiment showed that designing a good set of low-level heuristics is very important, a good set could give good results for any tested hyper-heuristics, even for a random roulette choice function, while an incorrectly composed set of primitive heuristics did not allow almost any algorithm to learn which heuristic to choose. The experiments on real DNA sequence instances pointed out two algorithms to be better than others: simulated annealing and the roulette choice function. In the comparison with other algorithms designed for that problem, the usage of elements from the spectrum in the solution was comparable with those obtained by hyper-heuristics, while the similarity of the solution and the examined DNA sequence was superior for tailored-to-measure algorithms.

4.3. DNA sequencing by hybridization, second approach

In Ref. [50], again the DNA sequencing by hybridization problem was considered, but this time accompanied by other combinatorial problems: the knapsack problem, traveling salesman problem (TSP) and its two variants, namely, bottleneck TSP and prize collecting TSP. For these problems, a few hyper-heuristics were implemented, similar to those presented in

Section 4.2 and [39]. It is not new that the same hyper-heuristic is used to solve problems in different domains. The novelty of the proposed approach was in modeling unified encoding of all the above problems, and implementing just one set of low-level heuristics. The heuristics were independent from the problems; thus, a domain barrier was moved down toward problems (compare **Figures 1** and **5**).

The solution for all the problems is represented as sequence S of integers from range 1 to n. For SBH, S denotes the elements of the spectrum, for TSPs, these are the cities to visit, and for the knapsack problem, S denotes the elements to be put to the bin of a given size. A few other data structures or variables were also used: distance matrix, prizes, and penalties, some of them redundant for a given problem, thus not used. The problems could be solved with the hyper-heuristic methods only due to using these specific representations and defining the evaluation function.

The proposed low-level heuristics were simple moves, however, taking into account the specificity of the tested problems. Besides the low-level heuristics previously proposed, insert, delete, swap, and shift, and four more were implemented: (i) replace an element from S with an element not being in S, (ii) move a few subsequent elements in the solution, (iii) revert the subsequence of elements in S, and (iv) remove the element from S which gives the highest cost to the preceding element in the solution, and replace it with the best one.

Some hyper-heuristics could distinguish, useless low-level heuristics or ones leading to unfeasible solutions, and discard them from further computations. The overall results were 'good enough', but with the increase of algorithm's generality, the quality of the obtained solution decreased a little in comparison to hyper-heuristics from Ref. [39] and other tailored metaheuristics.

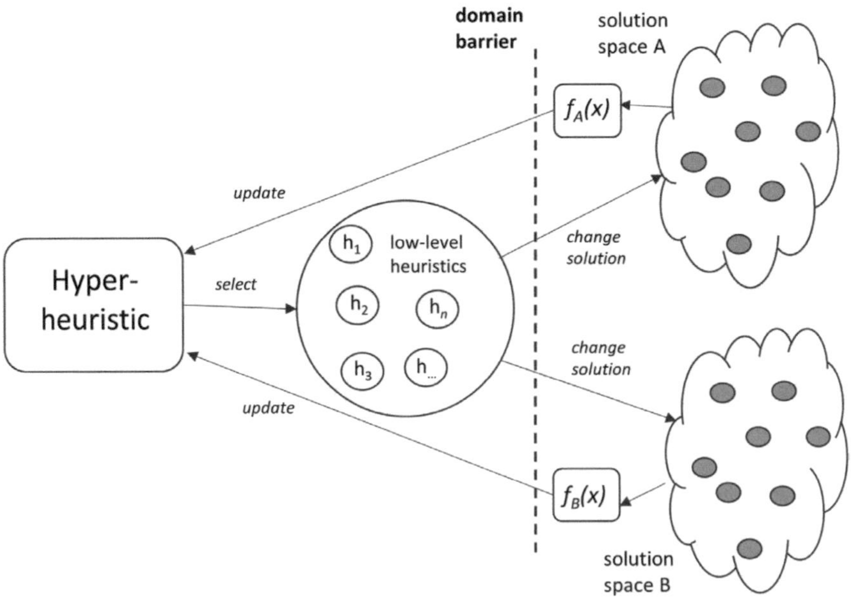

Figure 5. In the unified encoding of the hyper-heuristic scheme there is just one set of low-level heuristics for several problems, while in the standard scheme (**Figure 1**), for each problem, one must implement a separate set of heuristics.

5. Assembling a genome as a continuation of SBH ideas

The previous section presented a few bioinformatics problems solved with hyper-heuristics. Not many attempts have been made so far, due to the specificity of biological problems.

Sequencing by hybridization is a method that did not stand the test of time, but ideas developed in this approach can be translated into the next level of reading DNA sequences, namely assembling. The explosion of new technology allows to directly read short DNA fragments, up to a few hundreds of molecules, and thus making the old-fashioned and costly approaches, Sanger sequencing [51] and SBH, not useful anymore. The inputs to the assembly problem are these longer sequences merged in order to get a longer one of the size of a bacterial genome. In the 'toy problem' -SBH, the fragments are of a length of a dozen or so, and the solution sequence is a few hundred long, while for the assembly problem, DNA fragments are in the range 100–1000 molecules and are assembled into a million-molecule sequence. Both problems can be modeled as searching for a path in the graph, where nodes represent short DNA fragments, and arcs connect overlapping nodes with the cost equal to the shift between the two neighboring fragments. However, in DNA assembly, one must allow mismatches in fragment overlapping, differences in fragment lengths, and the fact that fragments may come from two strands of DNA helix; thus, they are reverse and complementary (the example of the reverse complementary sequence is presented in **Figure 6**). Also, the number of input fragments differs, a few hundred for SBH and millions for assembly. Moreover, during the process of reading DNA fragments, some parts of the genome could be poorly covered by the fragments or even in some cases not covered at all. There might be a few reasons for that, one of them, for example, depends on the content of G and C letters in the fragment of the genome. Thus, the assembly problem becomes much more difficult than SBH, and we cannot say any more about the 'ideal case' and 'easily solvable' problem.

The assembly problem is usually divided into three steps:

Step 1. Finding overlaps of input sequences; constructing a graph.

Step 2. Searching for a path in the graph.

Step 3. Building a consensus sequence.

In the first step, it is usually impossible to calculate the overlaps between each pair of fragments, due to a huge number of fragments and time limitations. In Step 2, instead of one path, the methods output few or more paths, because of sequencing errors, the lack of coverage, and the repetitions in the genome. The last step is the multiple sequence alignment problem, which again is not easily solvable. There are two main approaches to solve the DNA assembly problem. The first one, Overlap-Layout-Consensus (OLC), represents DNA fragments as nodes in the *overlap graph* (Step 1) and calculates in a smart way the overlaps of the fragments. The latter builds a *decomposition-based graph,* not quite precisely called de Bruijn graph, by putting k-mers on the nodes and decomposing each DNA fragment into a series of k-mers shifted by one. Hence, a DNA fragment, in this case, is represented as a path in the graph connecting a series of respective nodes. In the second case, there is no need to

Figure 6. An example of the reverse and complementary sequence. A DNA sequence is always read from 5′ end to 3′ end. Due to the complementarity rule, A on one strand is connected with T on the other, and G is connected with C. The following fragment of the DNA helix can be read as 'accgacttgcga' or 'tcgcaagtcggt'.

calculate overlaps between fragments, because they simply span the same nodes. On the other hand, a lot of information may be lost after decomposing a fragment into *k*-mers. The other two steps are similar for both approaches but take into account the specificity of each approach. There are many methods developed for both of the approaches: OLC [52, 53] and decomposition-based graphs [54, 55] as examples. None of them can be seen as a general process of a local search, where one could use a meta or hyper-heuristic method. Each step of the method is processed independently by a heuristic and/or a greedy approach. However, there is one place where an 'intelligent method', likely a hyper-heuristic, could be of value while searching for a path in the graph. The most difficult in the search process are junctions in the graph, which occur in the case of sequencing errors or repetitions. An example of a junction is presented in **Figure 7**. A hyper-heuristic which could distinguish in the search process that the path is coming to a junction and cut the current process would highly improve the solution. The method shall take into account the increase or decrease of the coverage and basing on this change and decide whether to stop or continue the search process. This must be preceded by offline training of many benchmark data sets, where a method could learn the specific cases in the graph and make predictions in the future search. The two basic steps that

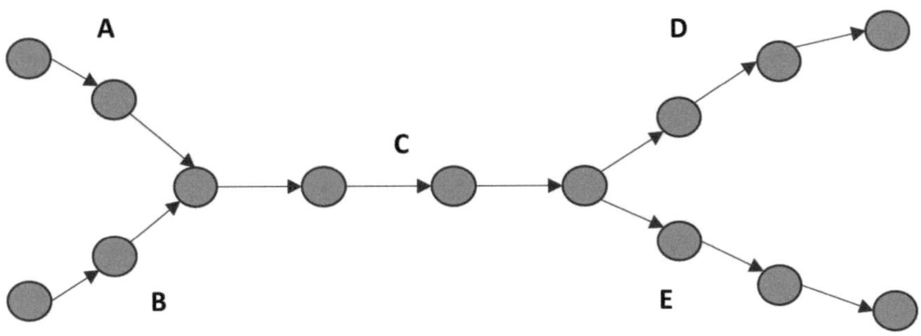

Figure 7. Junctions in the graph complicate the assembly process. In order to simplify the figure, only the arcs with the smallest shift between the two nodes are given. Without additional information, it is difficult to state if the correct sequence should be composed of fragments ACD, ACE, BCD, or BCE. Thus, the methods usually cut the current path and output shorter fragments like AC or CE.

a hyper-heuristic would choose could be a simple 'stop searching' and 'continue extending the path', but of course, many other heuristics like extending search path in both directions could also be added.

One may notice that the field of bioinformatics combinatorial optimization problems is not well explored in terms of hyper-heuristic search. The assembly problem is just one example of many problems, where a hyper-heuristic could be introduced. The question is if we are ready to allow a possible deterioration of the final solution by generalizing the search process. The other question is what is the most time-consuming activity: understanding a bio problem, designing a model, or implementing a method? In the case of some problems, it is crucial to clearly understand the problem because omitting some of the details makes the solution unacceptable for bio-experts. Hyper-heuristics and especially low-level heuristics should be developed to comply with all the restrictions and produce a feasible solution, which, unfortunately, in many cases may take as much time as implementing a 'tailored-to-measure' algorithm.

6. Summary and future

The flow of ideas between biology, operational research, and computer science works in both directions. The ideas from the biological evolution serve as the basis of genetic algorithms and genetic programming. The operational research models and methods help to solve many problems arising in computational biology. Recently, an interesting cooperation between these two scientific areas has been observed in the behavior of the slime mold *Physarum*, for which a mathematical model for the dynamics always converges in finding the shortest path for any input graph [56, 57]. There were also some attempts to involve DNA and use it as the computing power [58].

We can observe a constant synergy between specialists from different areas. This synergy can also be found in the context of hyper-heuristic methodology. It has been shown that hyper-heuristics have been successfully involved in solving several combinatorial optimization problems. Also, a few attempts have been made to solve bio-inspired problems: the longest common subsequence problem and sequencing by hybridization problem.

In Section 5, a proposition how to employ hyper-heuristic search also in solving the DNA assembly problem has been made. By allowing offline learning on some benchmark dataset, the method could distinguish the junctions of the path in the graph and react faster whether to extend or cut the current path.

A good learning mechanism incorporated into hyper-heuristics is a key to increase the usage of hyper-heuristics and to solve the problems in a competitive way to tailored-to-measure (meta)heuristics. In this context, the development of the tools for assessing hyper-heuristics such as HyFlex [59] or Hyperion [60] may increase the usage of these types of methods.

Acknowledgements

The author would like to thank J. Blazewicz, G. Felici and the anonymous referee for valuable remarks and the discussions which significantly improved the presentation of the paper.

The research was partially supported by a Poznan University of Technology grant [09/91/DSPB/0600].

Author details

Aleksandra Swiercz

Address all correspondence to: aswiercz@cs.put.poznan.pl

1 Institute of Computing Science, Poznan University of Technology, Poland

2 Institute of Bioorganic Chemistry, Polish Academy of Sciences, Poznań, Poland

References

[1] Cowling P, Kendall G, Soubeiga E. A hyperheuristic approach for scheduling a sales summit. In: Selected Papers of the 3rd International Conference on the Practice and Theory of Automated Timetabling, PATAT 2000. Berlin: Springer; 2001. pp. 176-190

[2] Fisher H, Thompson GL. Probabilistic learning combinations of local job-shop scheduling rules. In: Muth JF and Thompson GL, editors. Industrial Scheduling. NY: Prentice-Hall: Englewood Cliffs; 1963. pp. 225-251

[3] Storer RH, Wu SD, Vaccari R. New search spaces for sequencing problems with application to job shop scheduling. Management Science. 1992;**38**(10):1495-1509

[4] Fang H, Ross P, Corne D. A promising hybrid ga/heuristic approach for openshop scheduling problems. In: Cohn AG, editor. European Conference on Artificial Intelligence. New York: John Wiley & Sons; 1994

[5] Drechsler R, Becker B. Learning heuristics by genetic algorithms. In: Shirakawa I, editor. ASP Design Automation Conference. ACM: Makuhari, Massa, Chiba, Japan; 1995. pp. 349-352

[6] Grefenstette J. Optimization of control parameters for genetic algorithms. IEEE Transactions on Systems, Man, and Cybernetics SMC. 1986;**16**(1):122-128

[7] Bäck T. An overview of parameter control methods by self-adaption in evolutionary algorithms. Fundamental Journals. 1998;**35**(1-4):51-66

[8] Rice JR. The algorithm selection problem. Advances in Computers. 1976;**15**:65-118

[9] Sleeman D, Rissakis M, Craw S, Graner N, Sharma S, Consultant-2: Pre–and post-processing of machine learning applications. International Journal of Human Computer Studies. 1995;**43**(1):43-63

[10] Wah BW, Ieumwananonthachai A. Teacher: A genetics-based system for learning and for generalizing heuristics. In: Yao X, editor. Evolutionary Computation. Singapore: World Scientific Publishing Co. Pte. Ltd.; 1999. pp. 124-170

[11] Burke EK, Gendreau M, Hyde M, Kendall G, Ochoa G, Ozcan E, Qu R. Hyper-heuristics: A survey of the state of the art. Journal of the Operational Research Society. 2013;**64**:1695-1724

[12] Pappa GL, Ochoa G, Hyde MR, Freitas AA, Woodward J, Swan J. Genetic Programming and Evolvable Machines. Contrasting meta-learning and hyper-heuristic research: The role of evolutionary algorithms. 2014;**15**(1):3-35. DOI: 10.1007/s10710-013-9186-9

[13] Lysov Y, Florent'ev V, Khorlin A, Khrapko K, Shik V, Mirzabekov A, Determination of the nucleotide sequence of DNA using hybridization with oligonucleotides. A new method. Doklady Akademii Nauk SSSR. 1988;**303:**1508-1511

[14] Pevzner P, l-tuple DNA sequencing: Computer analysis. Journal of Biomolecular Structure and Dynamics. 1989;**7:**63-73

[15] Blazewicz J, Hertz A, Kobler D, de Werra D. On some properties of DNA graphs. Discrete Applied Mathematics. 1999;**98:**1-19

[16] Vrugt J, Robinson B. Improved evolutionary optimization from genetically adaptive multimethod search. Proceedings of the National Academy of Sciences. 2007;**104**(3):708-711

[17] Burke EK, Hyde M, Kendall G, Ochoa G, Özcan E, Woodward J. Handbook of metaheuristics, international series in operations research & management science. Vol. 146. Chap. A Classification of Hyper-heuristic Approaches, New York: Springer; 2010. pp. 449-468. Chapter 15

[18] Ahmadi S, Barrone P, Cheng P, Burke EK, Cowling P, McCollum B. Perturbation based variable neighbourhood search in heuristic space for examination timetabling problem. In: Kendall G, Burke EK, Petrovic S, Gendreau M, editors. Multidisciplinary International Scheduling: Theory and Applications. New York: MISTA, Springer; 2003. pp. 155-171

[19] Burke EK, McCollum B, Meisels A, Petrovic S, Qu R. A graph-based hyperheuristic for educational timetabling problems. European Journal of Operational Research. 2007; **176**:177-192

[20] Sabar NR, Ayob M, Qu R, Kendall G. A graph coloring constructive hyper-heuristic for examination timetabling problems. Applied Intelligence. 2012;**37:**1-11

[21] Cano-Belmán J, Ríos-Mercado R, Bautista J. A scatter search based hyperheuristic for sequencing a mixed-model assembly line. Journal of Heuristics. 2010;**16**:749-770

[22] Dowsland KA, Soubeiga E, Burke EK. A simulated annealing hyperheuristic for determining shipper sizes for storage and transportation. European Journal of Operational Research. 2007;**179**(3):759-774

[23] Pisinger D, Ropke S. A general heuristic for vehicle routing problems. Computers and Operations Research. 2007;**34**(8):2403-2435

[24] Pillay N. Evolving hyper-heuristics for the uncapacitated examination timetabling problem. In: Blazewicz J, Drozdowski M, Kendall G, McCollum B (eds). Multidisciplinary International Conference on Scheduling: Theory and Applications (MISTA'09). Dublin, Ireland; 2009. pp. 447-457

[25] Keller RE, Poli R. Cost-benefit investigation of a genetic-programming hyperheuristic. In: Monmarche' N, Talbi E-G, Collet P, Schoenauer M, Lutton E, editors. International Conference on Artificial Evolution. Berlin, Heidelberg: Springer-Verlag; 2007. pp. 13-24

[26] Runka A. Evolving an edge selection formula for ant colony optimization. In: Genetic and evolutionary computation conference (GECCO'09). New York: ACM; 2009. pp. 1075-1081

[27] Burke EK, Hyde MR, Kendall G. Evolving bin packing heuristics with genetic programming. In: Parallel Problem Solving from Nature PPSN IX, Lecture Notes in Computer Science. Runarsson T.P., Beyer HG, Burke E, Merelo-Guervós JJ, Whitley LD, Yao X (eds). Springer, Berlin, Heidelberg. Vol. 4193. 2006. pp. 860-869

[28] Burke EK, Hyde MR, Kendall G. Grammatical evolution of local search heuristics. IEEE Transactions on Evolutionary Computation. 2012;**16**:406-417

[29] Sim K, Hart E, Paechter B. A hyper-heuristic classifier for one dimensional bin packing problems: Improving classification accuracy by attribute evolution. In: Parallel Problem Solving from Nature: PPSN XII, Vol. 7492. Coello CAC, Cutello V, Deb K, Forrest S, Nicosia G, Pavone M. (eds). Lecture Notes in Computer Science. Springer, Berlin, Heidelberg. 2012. pp. 348-357

[30] Ross P, Marín-Blázquez JG. Constructive hyper-heuristics in class timetabling. In: IEEE Congress on Evolutionary Computation (CEC'05), Edinburgh, UK. 2005. pp. 1493-1500

[31] Burke EK, Petrovic S, Qu R. Case based heuristic selection for timetabling problems. Journal of Scheduling. 2006;**9**(2):115-132

[32] Fukunaga AS. Automated discovery of local search heuristics for satisfiability testing. Evolutionary Computation. 2008;**16**(1):31-61

[33] Burke EK, Hyde MR, Kendall G, Woodward J. Automating the packing heuristic design process with genetic programming. Evolutionary Computation. 2012;**20**(1):63-89

[34] Krasnogor N, Gustafson S. A study on the use of "self-generation" in memetic algorithms. Natural Computing. 2004;**3**(1):53-76

[35] Garrido P, Riff M. Dvrp: A hard dynamic combinatorial optimisation problem tackled by an evolutionary hyper-heuristic. Journal of Heuristics 2010;**16**:795-834

[36] Remde S, Cowling P, Dahal K, Colledge N. Binary exponential back-off for tabu tenure in hyperheuristics. In: Cotta C, Cowling P, editors. Evolutionary Computation in Combinatorial Optimization. Vol. 5482. Berlin: Springer; 2009. pp. 109-112

[37] Terashima-Marín H, Ross P, Farías-Zárate CJ, López-Camacho E, Valenzuela-Rendón M. Generalized hyper-heuristics for solving 2D regular and irregular packing problems. Annals of Operations Research 2010;**179**(1):369-392

[38] Rattadilok P, Gaw A, Kwan RSK. Distributed choice function hyper-heuristics for timetabling and scheduling. In: Burke EK, Trick M, editors. The Practice and Theory of Automated Timetabling V: Selected Papers from the 5th International Conference on the Practice and Theory of Automated Timetabling. Vol. 3616. Lecture Notes in Computer Science Series. Berlin: Springer; 2005. pp. 51-70

[39] Blazewicz J, Burke EK, Kendall G, Mruczkiewicz W, Oguz C, Swiercz A. A hyper-heuristic approach to sequencing by hybridization of DNA sequences. Annals of Operations Research. 2013;**207**(1):27-41. DOI: 10.1007/s10479-011-0927-y

[40] Nareyek A. An empirical analysis of weight-adaptation strategies for neighborhoods of heuristics. In: Sousa J, editor. Metaheuristic International Conference MIC'2001. Porto, Portugal. 2001. pp. 211-215

[41] Burke EK, Kendall G, Soubeiga E. A tabu-search hyperheuristic for timetabling and rostering. Journal of Heuristics. 2003;**9**(6):451-470

[42] Koza JR. Genetic Programming: On the Programming of Computers by Means of Natural Selection. Boston, MA: The MIT Press; 1992

[43] Ho NB and Tay JC. Evolving dispatching rules for solving the flexible job-shop problem. In: IEEE Congress on Evolutionary Computation (CEC'05). Edinburgh, UK: IEEE; 2005. pp. 2848-2855

[44] Poli R, Woodward JR and Burke EK. A histogram matching approach to the evolution of bin-packing strategies. In: IEEE Congress on Evolutionary Computation (CEC'07). Singapore: IEEE; 2007. pp. 3500-3507

[45] Oltean M, Dumitrescu D. Evolving TSP heuristics using multi expression programming. In: International Conference on Computational Science (ICCS'04). Vol. 3037. Lecture Notes in Computer Science. Berlin: Springer; 2004. pp. 670-673

[46] Weiss K, Khoshgoftaar TM, Wang DD. A survey of transfer learning. Journal of Big Data. 2016;**3**:9

[47] Sankoff D, Kruskal J. Time Warps, String Edits and Macromolecules: The Theory and Practice of Sequence Comparisons. Addison-Wesley. 1983

[48] Storer JA. Data Compression: Methods and theory. Computer Science Press Inc.; New York, NY, USA. 1988

[49] Tabataba FS, Mousavi SR. A hyper-heuristic for the longest common subsequence problem. Computational Biology and Chemistry. 2012;**36**:42-54

[50] Swiercz A, Burke EK, Cicheński M, Pawlak G, Petrovic S, Zurkowski T, Blazewicz J. Unified encoding for hyper-heuristics with application to bioinformatics. Central European Journal of Operations Research. 2014;**22**:567-589

[51] Sanger F, Nicklen S, Coulson A. DNA sequencing with chain-terminating inhibitors, Proceedings of the National Academy of Sciences, USA. 1977;**74**:5463-5467

[52] Myers E, Sutton G, Delcher A. A whole-genome assembly of Drosophila, Science. 2000; **287**(5461):2196-2204

[53] Simpson J, Durbin R. Efficient de novo assembly of large genomes using compressed data structures, Genome Research. 2012;**22**:549-556

[54] Zerbino D, Birney E. Velvet: Algorithms for de novo short read assembly using de Bruijn graphs, Genome Research. 2008;**18**:821-829

[55] Kajitani R, Toshimoto K, Noguchi H, Toyoda A, Ogura Y, Okuno M, Yabana M, Harada M, Nagayasu E, Maruyama H, Kohara Y, Fujiyama A, Hayashi T, Itoh T. Efficient de novo assembly of highly heterozygous genomes from whole-genome shotgun short reads, Genome Research. 2014;**24**:1384-1395

[56] Bonifaci V, Mehlhorn K, Varma G. Physarum can compute shortest paths. Journal of Theoretical Biology. 2012;**309**:121-133

[57] Bonifaci V. Physarum can compute shortest paths: A short proof. Information Processing Letters. 2013;**113**(1-2):4-7

[58] Adleman LM. Molecular computation of solutions to combinatorial problems. Science. 1994;**266**:1021-1024

[59] Ochoa G, Walker J, Hyde M, Curtois T. Adaptive evolutionary algorithms and extensions to the HyFlex hyper-heuristic framework. In: Parallel Problem Solving from Nature—PPSN XII. Lecture Notes in Computer Science. Berlin: Springer. 2012;**7492**:418-427

[60] Swan J, Özcan E, Kendall G. Hyperion—A recursive hyper-heuristic framework. In: Coello CAC, editor. LION. Lecture Notes in Computer Science. Berlin: Springer. 2011;**6683**:616-630

Chapter 2

Multi-Objective Hyper-Heuristics

Mashael Suliaman Maashi

Additional information is available at the end of the chapter

http://dx.doi.org/10.5772/intechopen.69222

Abstract

Multi-objective hyper-heuristics is a search method or learning mechanism that operates over a fixed set of low-level heuristics to solve multi-objective optimization problems by controlling and combining the strengths of those heuristics. Although numerous papers on hyper-heuristics have been published and several studies are still underway, most research has focused on single-objective optimization. Work on hyper-heuristics for multi-objective optimization remains limited. This chapter draws attention to this area of research to help researchers and PhD students understand and reuse these methods. It also provides the basic concepts of multi-objective optimization and hyper-heuristics to facilitate a better understanding of the related research areas, in addition to exploring hyper-heuristic methodologies that address multi-objective optimization. Some design issues related to the development of hyper-heuristic framework for multi-objective optimization are discussed. The chapter concludes with a case study of multi-objective selection hyper-heuristics and its application on a real-world problem.

Keywords: hyper-heuristics, multi-objective optimization, meta-heuristics, evolutionary algorithms, computational search problems

1. Introduction

Many real-world problems are complex. Owing to the (often) NP-hard nature of such problems, researchers and practitioners frequently resort to problem-tailored heuristics in order to obtain a reasonable solution within a reasonable amount of time. Hyper-heuristics are methodologies that operate on a search space of heuristics rather than directly searching the solution space for solving hard computational problems. One of the main aims of hyper-heuristics is to raise the level of generality of search methodologies and to automatically adapt the algorithm by combining the strength of each heuristic and making up for the weaknesses of others. References to multi-objective hyper-heuristics are scarce as most research in this area has been limited to single-objective optimization. The purpose of this chapter is to provide an introduction to hyper-heuristic methodologies that are designed for multi-objective optimization (HHMOs). The chapter might help researchers and PhD students interested in this research area to understand and use these methods. Hyper-heuristics for multi-objective optimization is a relatively new area of research in operational research (OR) and evolutionary computation [1, 2]. Few studies have dealt with hyper-heuristics for multi-objective problems. In order to offer a better understanding of the subject, the basic concepts of multi-objective optimization and hyper-heuristics are provided in Section 2. This chapter also provides a brief survey of hyper-heuristic methodologies that address multi-objective optimization in Section 3. Some design issues related to the development of a hyper-heuristic framework for multi-objective optimization are discussed in Section 4. Additionally, a case study of multi-objective selection hyper-heuristics and its application on a real-world problem is presented in Section 5. Finally, promising research areas for future application are provided in Section 6.

2. The basic concepts and underlying issues

2.1. Multi-objective optimization

Multi-objective problems (MOPs): MOPs comprise several objectives (two or more), which need to be minimized or maximized depending on the problem. A general definition of an MOP [3] is

An MOP minimizes $F(x) = (f_1(x), \ldots, f_k(x))$ subject to $g_i(x) \leq 0; i = 1, \ldots, m, x \in \Omega$. The solution of the MOP minimizes the components of a vector $F(x)$, where x is an n-dimensional decision variable vector $(X = x_1, \ldots, x_n)$ from some universe Ω. An MOP includes n decision variables, m constraints,and k objectives. The MOP's evaluation function $F: \Omega \rightarrow \Lambda$ maps decision variable vectors $(X = x_1, \ldots, x_n)$ to vectors $(Y = a_1, \ldots, a_k)$.

Multi-objective optimization techniques are divided into three classes [3, 4]:

- **A priori approach** (decision making and then a search):
  In this class, the objective preferences or weights are set by the decision maker prior to the search process. An example of this is aggregation-based approaches such as the weighted sum approach.
- **A posteriori approach** (a search and then decision making):
  The search is conducted to find solutions for the objective functions. Following this, a decision process selects the most appropriate solutions (often involving a trade-off). Multi-objective evolutionary optimization (MOEA) techniques, whether non-Pareto-based or Pareto-based, are examples of this class.
- **Interactive or progressive approach** (search and decision making simultaneously):
  In this class, the preferences of the decision maker(s) are made and adjusted during the search process.

Pareto dominance: The idea behind the dominance concept is to generate a preference between MOP solutions since there is no information regarding objective preference provided by the decision maker. This preference is used to compare the dominance between any two solutions [5]. A more formal definition of Pareto dominance (for minimization case) is as follows [4]:

A vector $u = (u_1, \ldots, u_k)$ is said to dominate another vector $v = (v_1, \ldots, v_k)$ (denoted by $u \precsim v$) according to k objectives if and only if u is partially less than v, that is, $\forall i \in \{1, \ldots, k\}, u_i \le v_i \wedge \exists i \in \{1, \ldots, k\}$ $: u_i < v_i$.

All non-dominated solutions are also known as the *Pareto optimal sets*. The corresponding Pareto optimal set, with respect to the objective space, is known as the *Pareto optimal front*. The quality of the obtained *Pareto optimal set* can be determined in Refs. [6, 7]: the extent of the Pareto optimal set and the distance and the distribution of the Pareto optimal front.

2.2. Hyper-heuristics

The main aim of the hyper-heuristic methodology is raising the level of generality of search techniques by producing general search algorithms that are applicable for solving a wide range of the problems in different domains [2, 8, 9]. In a hyper-heuristic approach, different heuristics (or heuristic components) can be selected, generated, or combined to solve a given optimization problem in an efficient way. Since each heuristic has its own strengths and weaknesses, one of the aims of hyper-heuristics is to automatically inform the algorithm by combining the strength of each heuristic and making up for the weaknesses of others. This process requires the incorporation of a learning mechanism into the algorithm to adaptively direct the search at each decision point for a particular state of the problem or the stage of search. It is obvious that the concept of hyper-heuristics has strong ties to operational research (OR) in terms of finding optimal or near-optimal solutions to computational search problems. It is also firmly linked to artificial intelligence (AI) in terms of machine-learning methodologies [8].

2.2.1. Generic hyper-heuristic framework

In their simplest form, hyper-heuristics is a search methodology that encompasses a high-level strategy (which could be a meta-heuristic) that controls the search over a set of heuristics (low-level heuristics) rather than controlling a search over a direct representation of the solutions. Usually, in a hyper-heuristic framework, there is a clear separation between high-level strategy and the set of low-level heuristics [10]. The purpose of domain barrier is to give the hyper-heuristics a higher level of abstraction. This also increases the level of generality of hyper-heuristics by enabling its application to a new problem without the need for a framework change. Only information relevant to the problem domain is provided from low level to high level, including cost/fitness measured by an evaluation function, indicating the quality of a solution. The high-level strategy can be a (meta-) heuristic or a learning mechanism. The task of the high-level strategy is to guide the search intelligently and adapt according to the success/failure of the low-level heuristics or combinations of heuristic components during the search process.

2.2.2. Hyper-heuristics classification

Generally, there are two recognized methodologies of hyper-heuristics: *selection* and *generation* hyper-heuristics. For both hyper-heuristic methodologies, there are two types of heuristics: (i) *constructive heuristics*, which process a partial solution(s) and build a complete solution(s) and (ii) *perturbative heuristics*, which operate on complete solution(s).

In the context of hyper-heuristics for multi-objective optimization, we could classify them into three categories:

- **Multi-objective selection hyper-heuristic** manages a number of heuristics during an iterative process for a given time. At each iteration, one of best heuristics is chosen at a decision point to operate and run. This type comprises two main stages: *heuristic selection* and *move-acceptance* strategy.
- **Multi-objective combination/hybridization hyper-heuristic** combines a number of heuristics or (components of heuristics) that operate simultaneously and adaptively to create new solutions.
- **Multi-objective generation hyper-heuristic:** To the best of the authors' knowledge, there are no studies addressing multi-objective generation hyper-heuristic in the literature.

3. Brief survey of hyper-heuristics for multi-objective optimization

The hyper-heuristics for multi-objective optimization problems is a new area of research in evolutionary computation and operational research [2, 8]. To date, few studies have been identified that deal with hyper-heuristics for multi-objective problems (see **Table 1**).

Regarding multi-objective selection hyper-heuristics, a multi-objective hyper-heuristic tabu search (TS) based (TSRoulette Wheel) was presented in Ref. [11]. In this approach, an appropriate heuristic is selected at each iteration using tabu search as a high-level search strategy. The experiments showed results with acceptable solution when applied in space allocation and timetabling problems. In Ref. [12], an online selection hyper-heuristic, Markov-chain-based hyper-heuristic (MCHH), is investigated. The Markov chain guides the selection of heuristics and applies online reinforcement learning to adapt transition weights between heuristics. In MCHH, hybrid meta-heuristics and evolution strategies were incorporated and applied to the DTLZ test problems [13] and compared to a (1+1) evolution strategy meta-heuristic, a random hyper-heuristic, and TSRoulette Wheel [11]. The comparison shows the efficacy of the proposed approach in terms of Pareto convergence and learning ability to select good heuristic combinations. Further work is needed in terms of diversity-preserving mechanisms. The MCHH was applied to the Walking Fish Group (WFG) test problems [14], and although the results from the performed tests show the ability of the approach, future work needs to be made to improve the search strategies [12]. MCHH has been applied to real-world water distribution networks and it produced competitive results [15]. A multi-objective hyper-heuristic optimization scheme for engineering system designs is presented in Ref. [16].

Component name	Application domain/test problems	Reference(s)
Tabu search	Space allocation, timetabling	[8]
	Traveling salesman problems	[35]
Markov chain, evolution strategy	Real-world water distribution networks design/DTLZ, WFG	[12]
NSGAII	Irregular 2D cutting stock	[37]
	Strip packing and cutting stock	[39]
NSGAII, quasi-Newton algorithm	Stacked neural network	[40]
Number of operations from NSGAII, SPEA2, and IBEA	A number of continuous multi-objective test problems	[19]
Number of selection, crossover, and mutation operations of evolutionary algorithms	Software module clustering	[23]
Hypervolume	Dynamic-mapped island-based model/WFG	[36]
Particle swarm optimization, adaptive metropolis algorithm, differential evolution	Water resource problems/a number of continuous multi-objective test problems	[41]
Memory strategy, genetic and differential operators	Dynamic optimization problems/a number of continuous multi-objective test problems	[46]
Genetic algorithm, simulated annealing, particle swarm optimization	Engineering system design problems/a number of classical multi-objective test problems	[16]
Simulated annealing	Shelf-space allocation	[34]
NSGAII, SPEA2,MOGA, choice function, great deluge algorithm, and late acceptance	WFG/the vehicle crashworthiness design problem	[24–26]
NSGAII, SPEA2, IBEA, choice function, great deluge algorithm	WFG/wind farm layout optimization	[32]
Markov model	DTLZ	[33]

Table 1. Heuristic components and application domains of hyper-heuristics for multi-objective optimization.

Simulated annealing (SA) [17], genetic algorithm, and particle swarm optimization [18] are used as low-level heuristics. A multi- indicator hyper-heuristics for multi-objective optimization is proposed in Ref. [19]. The approach based on multiple rank of indicators is taken from NSGAII [20], SPEA2 [22], and IBEA [21]. In Ref. [23], a multi-objective hyper-heuristic genetic algorithm (MHypGA) for multi-objective software module clustering problem is presented. In MHypGA, different strategies of selection, crossover, and mutation operations of genetic algorithms are incorporated as low-level heuristics. In Refs. [24–26], online-learning multi-objective hyper-heuristics are presented. These multi-objective hyper-heuristics are based on a choice function. The multi-objective choice-function-based hyper-heuristics are combined with different move-acceptance strategies including all-moves (AMs) and the great deluge algorithm (GDA) [27] and late acceptance (LA) [28]. The multi-objective hyper-heuristic controls and combines the strengths of three well-known multi-objective evolutionary algorithms (NSGAII [20], SPEA2 [22], and MOGA [30]). The performance of the proposed multi-objective choice-function-based hyper-heuristics is evaluated on the Walking Fish Group (WFG) test suite [14] and is applied to the vehicle crashworthiness design problem [31]. The results of both benchmark test problems demonstrate the capability and potential of the multi-objective hyper-heuristic approaches in solving continuous multi-objective optimization problems. More details about these approaches are provided as a study case in Section 5. In Ref. [32], a multi-objective selection hyper-heuristics for a multi-objective wind farm layout optimization is proposed. The experiential results show that the proposed approach is successfully applied to this optimization problem. In Ref. [33], a multi-objective selection sequence-based hyper-heuristic (MOSSHH) is proposed. The MOSSHH algorithm employs a hidden Markov model based on a sequence of heuristics that is determined by transition probabilities on ε-dominance. The proposed approach has been applied to DTLZ test problems [13] and results showed its capability to solve it through the learning process. A multiple neighborhood hyper-heuristic for two-dimensional (2D) shelf-space allocation problem is proposed in Ref. [34]. The proposed hyper-heuristic is based on a simulated annealing algorithm. A two-stage multi-objective hyper-heuristic approach is presented in Ref. [35]. The first phase targets in producing an efficient Pareto front, and the second phase focuses on solving a given problem in a flexible way so as to drive a subset of the population to the desired Pareto front. The approach was assessed on the multi-objective-traveling salesman problems using 11 low-level heuristics. Comparison with other methods from the scientific literature revealed that the proposed approach produces high-quality results. Nevertheless, upcoming efforts are still necessary in advancing the approach. In Ref. [36], a hypervolume-based hyper-heuristic for a dynamic-mapped multi-objective island-based model is proposed. This method shows its superiority when compared to the contribution-based hyper-heuristic and other standard parallel models over the WFG test problems [14]. A new hyper-heuristic based on the multi-objective evolutionary algorithm NSGAII [20] is proposed in Ref. [37]. The main idea of this method involves the production of the final Pareto-optimal set, through a learning process that evolves combinations of condition-action rules based on NSGAII. The proposed method was tested on many instances of irregular 2D-cutting stock benchmark problems and produced promising results. A hyper-heuristic-based codification is proposed in Refs. [38, 39], for solving strip packing and cutting stock problems in order to maximize the total profit and minimize the total number of cuts. The experimental results show that outcomes of the proposed hyper-heuristic outperform single heuristics. In Ref. [40], a multi-objective hyper-heuristic for the design and optimization of a stacked neural network is proposed. The proposed approach is based on NSGAII [20] combined with a local search algorithm (Quasi-Newton algorithm).

Regarding multi-objective hybridization hyper-heuristic, an adaptive multi-method (multi-point) search called AMALGAM is proposed in Ref. [41]. It employs multiple search algorithms, NSGAII [20], PSO [18], AMS [42], and DE [43], simultaneously using the concepts of multi-method search and adaptive offspring creation. AMALGAM has been applied to a number of continuous multi-objective test problems, and it has been shown to be superior to other methods. It has also been applied to solve a number of water resource problems and has yielded very good solutions [44, 45]. A multi-strategy ensemble, multi-objective evolutionary algorithm called MS-MOEA for dynamic optimization, is proposed in Ref. [46]. The approach combines differential operators and different strategies, including strategy and genetic, to adoptively creating offspring and increase the convergence speed. The results show that MS-MOEA obtains solution with good quality.

It is worth mentioning that multi-objective hybridization hyper-heuristics are similar to multi-objective selection hyper-heuristics in terms of the incorporation of different algorithms. However, they are different in their concepts. Multi-objective selection hyper-heuristic is based on two successive stages: a selection mechanism and an acceptance move strategy. By contrast, multi-objective hybridization hyper-heuristics is based on an adaptive creation offspring strategy. In multi-objective selection hyper-heuristics, a sequence of heuristics/meta-heuristics is executed during the search, that is, one heuristic/meta-heuristic is selected and applied at each stage (iteration/decision point) of the search. The high-level strategy in hyper-heuristics evaluates the performance of a set of heuristics/meta-heuristics in order to improve the population of solutions. By contrast, in multi-objective hybridization hyper-heuristics, multiple heuristic/meta-heuristics run concurrently. Each heuristic/meta-heuristic produces a different population of offspring, and then, all produced offspring are evaluated to evolve a new population of offspring by an adaptive creation offspring strategy.

4. Multi-objective hyper-heuristics design issues

The idea of hybridizing a number of algorithms (heuristics) into a hyper-heuristic framework is straightforward and meaningful. However, many design issues related to the development of hyper-heuristics for multi-objective optimization require more attention when designing such a framework to be applicable and effective.

The main components of the hyper-heuristic framework are low-level heuristics, selection method, learning mechanism, and move-acceptance method. The choosing of these components is critical. Each component in the hyper-heuristic framework plays a significant role in improving the quality of both the search and the eventual solution. The components of the hyper-heuristic in the context of multi-objective optimization are discussed as follows.

4.1. Low-level heuristics

The choice of appropriate low-level heuristics is not an easy task. Many questions arise here, what heuristics (algorithms) are suitable for dealing with multi-objective optimization problems? Are priori approaches or a posteriori approaches more suitable? Are non-Pareto-based or Pareto-based approaches more applicable? The author agrees with many researchers [30, 38, 47–51] that evolutionary algorithms and population-based methods such as decomposition-based approaches MOEA/Ds (e.g., [52, 53]) and indicator-based approaches (e.g., [54, 55] are more suitable in dealing with multi-objective optimization problems because of their population-based nature, which means that they can find Pareto optimal sets (trade-off solutions) in a single run, thus allowing a decision maker to select a suitable compromise solution (with respect to the space of the solutions). In the context of multi-objective hyper-heuristics, a decision maker here could be a selection method that decides which is the best low-level heuristic to select at each decision point (with respect to the space of the heuristics).

4.2. Selection methods

As a selection hyper-heuristic relies on an iterative process, the main questions arising here are what is an effective way to choose an appropriate heuristic at each decision point, and how to choose this heuristic, that is, which criteria can be considered when choosing a heuristic? In single-objective cases, this criterion is easy to determine by measuring the quality of the solution, such as the objective/cost value and time. However, this is more complex when tackling a multi-objective problem. The quality of the solution is not easy to assess. There are many different criteria that should be considered, such as the number of non-dominated individuals and the distance between the non-dominated front and the POF. To make a simple framework, a higher level of abstraction of the hyper-heuristics should be considered when designing such a framework. It is not necessary to provide any problem-specific information, such as the number of objectives or the nature of the solution space to the high-level strategy. More attention should be given to the performance of the low-level heuristics. This will boost the intensification element. Therefore, a heuristic with the best performance will be chosen more frequently to exploit the search area. The aim is to achieve a kind of balance between the intensification and diversification when choosing a heuristic. Selection methods based on randomization support only the diversification by exploring unvisited areas of the search space. Reinforcement learning (RL) [56] uses support intensification as a selection method by rewarding and punishing each heuristic based on its performance during the search using a scoring mechanism. An example of good selection method is the choice function, which could provide a balance between intensification and diversification.

4.3. Learning and feedback mechanism

Not all hyper-heuristic approaches incorporate a learning mechanism. However, a learning mechanism is strongly linked to the selection method. An example of this is a random hyper-heuristic classified as an offline-learning approach [1], because the random selection does not provide any kind of learning. The learning mechanism guides the selection method to which best heuristic should be chosen at each decision point. A best heuristic refers to the heuristic that produces solutions with good quality based on some criteria using performance measurements. It is good to note that the measurement of the quality of the solution for multi-objective problems requires assessing different aspects of the non-dominated set in the objective space. In the scientific literature, many performance metrics have been proposed to measure different aspects of the quality and quantity of the resulting non-dominated set [4, 29, 57].

4.4. Move-acceptance method

The selection hyper-heuristic framework comprises two main stages: selection and move-acceptance methods. A move-acceptance criterion can be deterministic or non-deterministic. A deterministic move-acceptance criterion produces the same result, given the configuration (e.g., proposed new solution, etc.). Non-deterministic move-acceptance criteria may generate a different result even when the same solutions are used for the decision at a same given time. This could be because the move-acceptance criterion depends on time or it might have a stochastic component while making the accept/reject decision. Examples of deterministic move-acceptance criteria are all-moves, only-improving, and improving & equal. For non-deterministic move-acceptance criteria, the candidate solution is always accepted if it improves the solution quality, while worsening solutions can be accepted based on an acceptance function, including GDA [27], LA [28], Monte Carlo [58], and SA [17]. Selection of the move-acceptance criteria has to be compatible with the selection methods. In the scientific literature, many combinations of the selection method and move-acceptance criterion have been successfully applied to single-objective optimization [59]. It could be worth employing them in the context of hyper-heuristics for multi-objective optimization.

5. Case study: multi-objective choice-function-based hyper-heuristics

5.1. The proposed multi-objective hyper-heuristics methodologies

This study [26] highlights the lack of scientific study that has been conducted in hyper-heuristics and multi-objective optimization, investigates the design of a hyper-heuristic framework for multi-objective optimization, and develops hyper-heuristic approaches for multi-objective optimization (HHMOs) to solve continuous multi-objective problems. Hyper-heuristic frameworks generally impose a domain barrier that separates the hyper-heuristic from the domain implementation along with low-level heuristics to provide a higher level of abstraction. The domain barrier does not allow any problem-specific information to be passed to the hyper-heuristic itself during the search process. The multi-objective choice-function-based hyper-heuristic framework is designed in this same modular manner (see **Figure 1**).

One of the advantages of the multi-objective choice-function-based hyper-heuristic framework is its simplicity. It is also highly flexible, and its components are reusable. Moreover, it is built on an interface that allows other researchers to write their own multi-objective hyper-heuristic components easily. Even the low-level heuristics can be easily changed if required. If new and better-performing components are found in the future, they can be incorporated. Based on the multi-objective selection hyper-heuristic framework, three online-learning-selection, choice-function-based hyper-heuristics are proposed: HHMO_CF_AM, HHMO_CF_GDA, and HHMO_CF_LA [24, 25]. The multi-objective choice-function-based hyper-heuristics control and combine the strengths of three well-known multi-objective evolutionary algorithms (NSGAII, SPEA2, and MOGA), which are -utilized as the low-level heuristics. The choice-function-selection heuristic acts as a high-level strategy that adaptively ranks the performance of those low-level heuristics according to feedback received during the search process, determining which one to call at each decision point. Four performance measurements (algorithm effort (AE), ratio of non-dominated individuals (RNI) [5], size of space covered (SSC) [60], and uniform distribution of a non-dominated population (UD) [61]) are integrated into a ranking scheme that acts as a feedback-learning mechanism

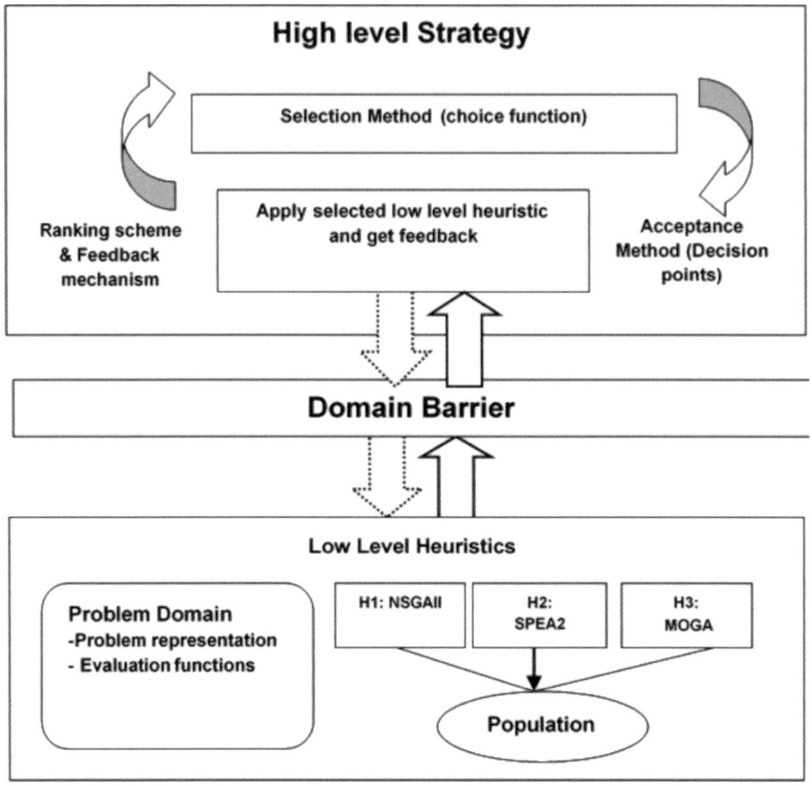

Figure 1. Proposed framework of the hyper-heuristic choice function based on multi-objective optimization problems.

to provide knowledge of the problem domain to the high-level strategy. The multi-objective choice-function-based hyper-heuristic is combined with different move-acceptance strategies, including all-moves (AM) as a deterministic move acceptance and GDA [27] and LA [28] as a non-deterministic move acceptance. GDA and LA require a change in the value of a single objective at each step, and hence a well-known hypervolume metric, referred to as D metric, is proposed for their applicability to the multi-objective optimization problems. The D metric is integrated into the non-deterministic move-acceptance criterion in order to convert the multi-objective optimization to the single-objective optimization without having to define value weights for the various objectives. For more details about the HHMOs algorithm, see Refs. [24, 25].

5.2. Problem description

The multi-objective vehicle crashworthiness design problem has only five decision variables and no constraints [31]. The output of the problem provides a wider choice for engineers to make their final design decision based on the Pareto solution space. The decision variables of the problem represent the thickness of five reinforced members around the front as they could have a significant effect on the crash safety. The mass of the vehicle is tackled as the first design objective, while the integration of collision acceleration between $t_1 = 0.05$ s and $t_2 = 0.07$ s in the full-frontal crash is considered as the second objective function. The toe-board intrusion in the 40% offset-frontal crash is tackled as the third objective as it is the most severe mechanical injury. The three objectives are formulated as follows:

$$\text{Mass} = 1640.2823 + 2.3573285\,t_1 - 2.3220035\,t_2 + 4.5688768\,t_3 + 7.7213633\,t_4 + 4.4559504\,t_5 \quad (1)$$

$$\begin{aligned}\text{Ain} = {} & 6.5856 + 1.15\,t_1 - 1.0427\,t_2 + 0.9738\,t_3 + 0.8364\,t_4 - 0.3695\,t_1 t_4 + 0.0861\,t_1 t_5 \\ & + 0.3628\,t_2 t_4 - 0.1106\,t_1^2 - 0.3437\,t_3^2 + 0.1764\,t_4^2\end{aligned} \quad (2)$$

$$\begin{aligned}\text{Intrusion} = {} & -0.0551 + 0.0181\,t_1 + 0.1024\,t_2 + 0.0421\,t_3 - 0.0073\,t_1 t_2 + 0.024\,t_2 t_3 \\ & - 0.0118\,t_2 t_4 - 0.0204\,t_3 t_4 - 0.008\,t_3 t_5 - 0.0241\,t_2^2 + 0.0109\,t_4^2\end{aligned} \quad (3)$$

Thus, the multi-objective design of vehicle crashworthiness problem in T decision variable space is formulated as

$$\begin{aligned} m \in F(x) &= [\text{Mass, Ain, Intrusion}] \\ s.t. 1\ \text{mm} &\le x \le 3\ \text{mm} \\ \textit{where } x &= (t_1, t_2, t_3, t_4, t_5)^T \end{aligned} \quad (4)$$

5.3. Performance evaluation criteria and experimental settings

A set of experiments are conducted over a multi-objective vehicle crashworthiness design problem as a real-world problem to evaluate the performance of the multi-objective choice-function-based hyper-heuristics: HHMO_CF_AM, HHMO_CF_GDA, and HHMO_CF_LA. The performance of three multi-objective hyper-heuristics is compared to the well-known multi-objective evolutionary algorithm, NSGAII [20]. Five performance metrics are used to measure the quality of the approximation sets from different aspects: (i) RNI [5], (ii) SSC [60], (iii) UD [61], (iv) generational distance (GD) [62], and (v) inverted generational distance (IGD) [63]. In addition, the *t*-test is used as a statistical test for the average performance comparison of selection hyper-heuristics and the results. Thirty independent runs are performed for each comparison method using the same parameter settings as those provided in Ref. [31] with a population size equal to 30. All multi-objective hyper-heuristics methodologies run for a total of 75 iterations (stages). In each iteration, a low-level heuristic is selected and applied to execute 50 generations. Thus, all methods are terminated after 3750 generations. Other experimental settings are provided in Refs. [24, 25].

5.4. Results

The mean performance comparison of AM, GDA, LA, and NSGAII based on the performance metrics (RNI, SSC, UD, GD, and IGD) for solving the vehicle crashworthiness problems is provided in **Tables 2** and **3**.

Method	RNI				SSC				UD			
	AVG	MIN	MAX	STD	AVG	MIN	MAX	STD	AVG	MIN	MAX	STD
NSGAII	**1.00**	1.00	1.00	**0.00**	7.936E+07	4.168E+07	9.587E+07	1.595E+07	0.592	0.532	0.670	0.045
AM	**1.00**	1.00	1.00	**0.00**	7.381E+07	5.315E+07	9.577E+07	**1.463E+07**	0.585	0.516	0.707	0.050
GDA	**1.00**	1.00	1.00	**0.00**	**8.289E+07**	6.294E+07	9.580E+07	1.954E+07	**0.613**	0.555	0.692	**0.034**
LA	**1.00**	1.00	1.00	**0.00**	7.538E+07	4.512E+07	9.550E+07	1.474E+07	0.582	0.302	0.641	0.062

Table 2. The performance NSGAII and the selection choice-function-based hyper-heuristics using different move-acceptance strategies on the vehicle crashworthiness problems with respect to the metrics: the ratio of non-dominated individuals (RNI), the hypervolume (SSC), and the uniform distribution (UD).

Method	GD				IGD			
	AVG	MIN	MAX	STD	AVG	MIN	MAX	STD
NSGAII	2.48E-03	1.46E-03	4.21E-03	9.10E-04	4.156E-03	1.543E-03	1.289E-02	3.859E-03
AM	2.71E-03	1.59E-03	4.06E-03	7.90E-04	4.376E-03	1.738E-03	1.288E-02	4.168E-03
GDA	**2.11E-03**	1.10E-03	4.28E-03	**7.10E-04**	**3.552E-03**	1.661E-03	1.230E-02	3.075E-03
LA	3.32E-03	1.70E-03	6.76E-03	1.33E-03	3.604E-03	1.525E-03	1.238E-02	**2.582E-03**

Table 3. The performance NSGAII and the selection choice-function-based hyper-heuristics using different move-acceptance strategies on the vehicle crashworthiness problems with respect to the metrics: the generational distance (GD) and the inverted generational distance (IGD).

For each performance metric, the average, minimum, maximum, and standard deviation values are computed. For all metrics, a higher value indicates better performance, except in GD and IGD, where a lower value indicates better performance. The statistical *t*-test results of NSGAII and the three multi-objective choice-function-based hyper-heuristics (AM, GDA, and LA) are given in **Table 4**.

The distribution of the simulation data of the 30 independent runs for the comparison methods with respect to these performance metrics is visualized as box plots, shown in **Figure 2**. The results indicate that all methods perform similar to each other with respect to the metric of RNI over. GDA exhibits the best performance in the metrics of SSC, GD, and IGD, and it converges better toward the POF than the other methods. GDA also exhibits the best performance in the metric of UD and distributes more uniformly than other methods.

The 50% attainment surface for each method, from the 30 fronts after 3750 generations, is computed and illustrated in **Figure 3**. GDA appears to generate a good convergence. It can be clearly observed that GDA converges to the best POF with a well-spread Pareto front as compared to the other approaches. By contrast, AM generates the poorest solutions. NSGAII and LA have similar convergence. In general, the hyper-heuristics for real-world multi-objective problems benefits from the use of a learning heuristic selection method as well as GDA. The results demonstrate the effectiveness of our selection hyper-heuristics particularly when combined with great deluge algorithm as a move-acceptance criterion. HHMO_CF_GDA

Methods	Metrics				
	RNI	SSC	UD	GD	IGD
NSGAII:AM	n/a	+	±	±	±
NSGAII:GDA	n/a	−	+	±	−
NSGAII:LA	n/a	+	+	+	−
AM:GDA	n/a	−	−	±	−
AM:LA	n/a	−	±	+	−
GDA:LA	n/a	+	+	+	±

Table 4. The *t*-test results of NSGAII and the three multi-objective choice-function-based hyper-heuristics methodologies on the multi-objective vehicle crashworthiness design problems with respect to the metrics: the ratio of non-dominated individuals (RNI), the hypervolume (SSC), the uniform distribution (UD), the generational distance (GD), and the inverted generational distance (IGD).

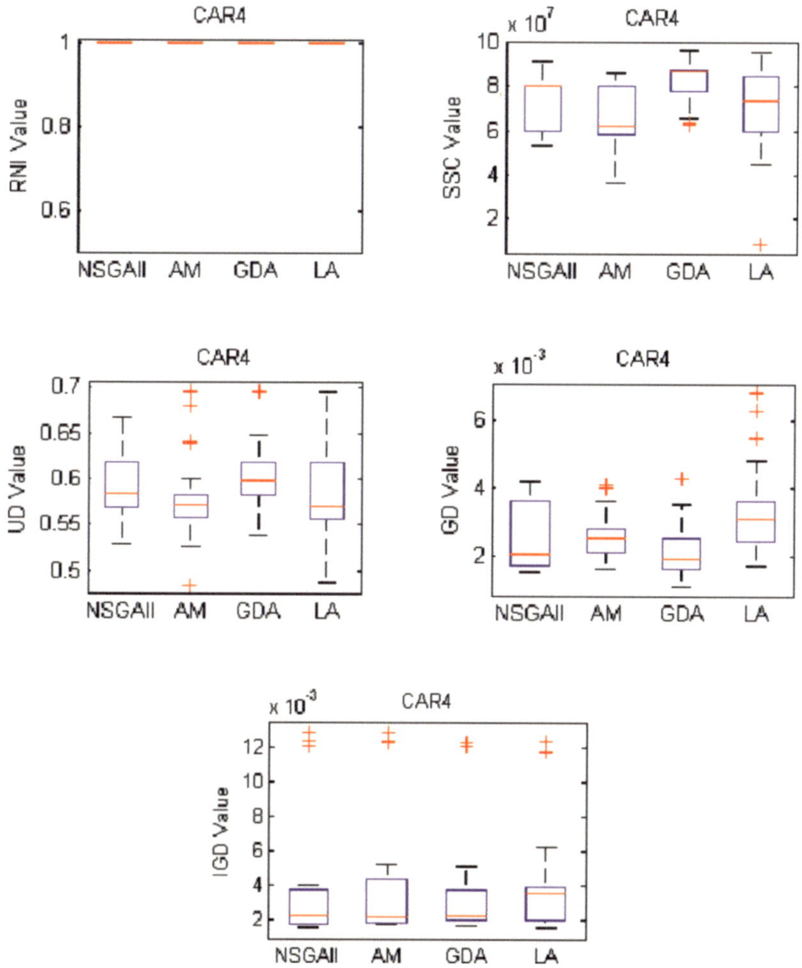

Figure 2. Box plots of multi-objective choice-function-based hyper-heuristics methodologies and NSGAII on the multi-objective vehicle crashworthiness design problems.

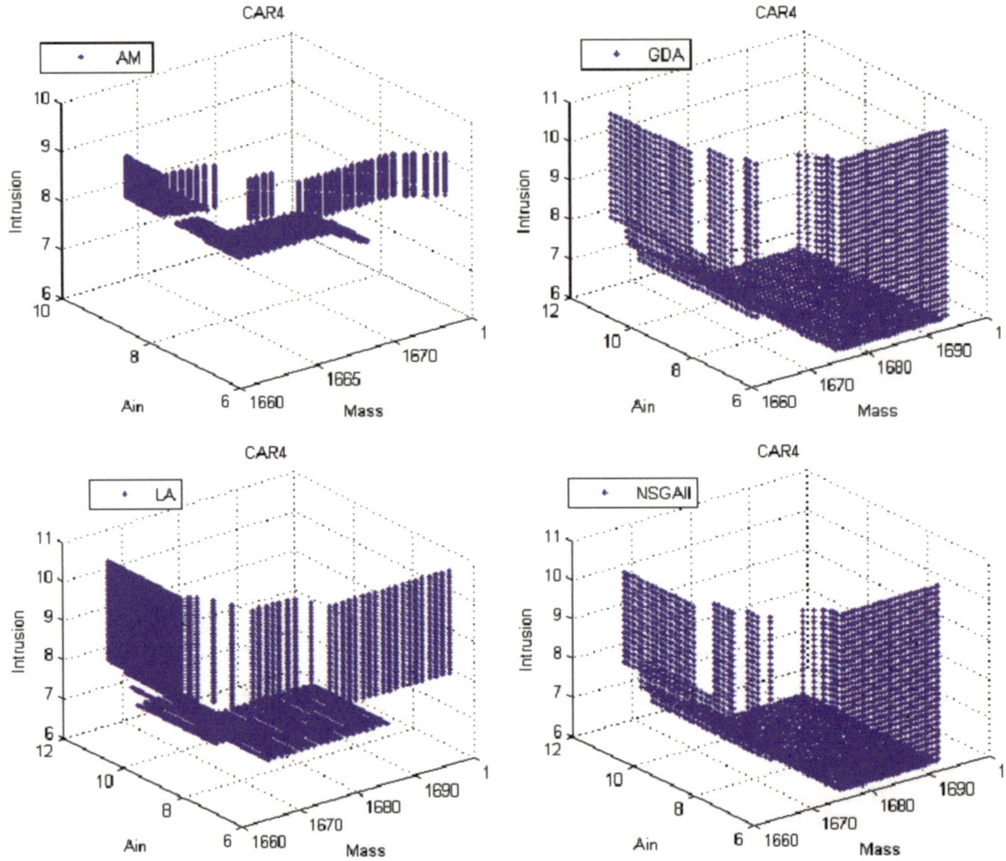

Figure 3. The 50% attainment surfaces for NSGAII and the three multi-objective choice-function-based hyper-heuristics (AM, GDA, and LA) after 3750 generations on the multi-objective design of vehicle crashworthiness problem.

turns out to be the best choice for solving this problem. Although other multi-objective hyper-heuristics still produce solutions with acceptable quality in some cases, they could not perform as well as NSGAII. In summary, the results of the real-world problem demonstrate the capability and potential of the multi-objective hyper-heuristic approaches in solving continuous multi-objective optimization problems.

6. Some promising research area

Multi-objective hyper-heuristic offers interesting potential research directions in multi-objective optimization. Some of these promising research areas are recommended as follows:

- Many heuristic selection methods can be adapted from previous research in single-objective optimization and can be used for multi-objective optimization within multi-objective selection hyper-heuristic. This process is not a trivial process, requiring elaboration of existing methods and their usefulness in a multi-objective setting. Furthermore, other acceptance criteria such as simulated annealing (SA) and tabu search (TS) [58] could be employed as a move-acceptance component within the selection hyper-heuristic framework for multi-objective optimization. As those criteria involve many parameters, this methodology would require initial experiments to tune the parameters for multi-objective settings, such as defining a cooling schedule and an initial temperature for SA and aspiration criterion and tabu tenure for TS.

- There are many low-level heuristics choices possible and, therefore, great scope for research in this area. It would be interesting to employ *state-of-the-art* multi-objective optimizers and other population-based methods that obtain promising results to act as low-level heuristics within the multi-objective combination/selection hyper-heuristic framework.
- It would be interesting to test the level of generality of existing multi-objective hyper-heuristic frameworks further on some other problems and domains, including the continuous real-valued constrained, combinatorial, discrete, and dynamic problems.
- Since no studies are found in the scientific literature that address multi-objective generation hyper-heuristic, it would be interesting to propose a multi-objective generation hyper-heuristic framework. This indicates great scope for research. Many-generation hyper-heuristic methodologies have been successfully applied to single-objective optimization; it would also be interesting to modify them to deal with multi-objective optimization.

Author details

Mashael Suliaman Maashi

Address all correspondence to: m.maashi@gmail.com

Tabuk University, King Saud University, Saudi Arabia

References

[1] Burke E, Hyde M, Kendall G, Ochoa G, Özcan E, Woodward JR. A classification of hyper-heuristic approaches. In: Handbook of Meta-Hruristics. USA: Kluwer Academic Publisher; 2010. pp. 449-468

[2] Özcan E, Bilgin B, Korkmaz, E. A comprehensive analysis of hyper-heuristics. Intelligent Data Analysis. 2008;**12**(1):3-23

[3] Van Veldhuizen DV, Lamont G. Multiobjective evolutionary algorithms: Analyzing the state-of-the-art. Evolutionary Computation. 2000;**8**(2):125-147

[4] Coello CC, Van Veldhuizen DV, Lamont G, editors. Evolutionary Algorithms for Solving Multi-Objective Problems. USA: Kluwer Academic Publishers; 2007

[5] Tan KC, Lee TH, Khor EF. Evolutionary algorithms for multi-objective optimization: Performance assessments and comparisons. Artificial Intelligence Review. 2002;**17**:253-290

[6] Landa-Silva D, Burke E, Petrovic S. An introduction to multiobjective metaheuristics for scheduling and timetabling. In: Lecture Notes in Economics and Mathematical Systems. Berlin, Heidelberg: Springer; 2004. pp. 91-129

[7] Zitzler E, Deb K, Thiele L. Comparison of multiobjective evolutionary algorithms: Empirical results. Evolutionary Computation. 2000;**8**(2):173-195

[8] Burke EK, Gendreau M, Hyde M, Kendall G, Ochoa G, Özcan E, Qu R. Hyper-heuristics: A survey of the state of the art. Journal of the Operational Research Society. 2013;**64**:1695-1724

[9] Ross P. Hyper-heuristics. In: Search Methodologies: Introductory Tutorials in Optimization and Decision Support Methodologies. Bücher: Springer; 2005. pp. 529-556

[10] Burke E, Kendall G, Newall J, Hart E, Ross P, Schulenburg S. Hyper-heuristics: An emerging direction in modern search technology. In: Handbook of Meta-Heuristics. USA: Kluwer Academic Publishers; 2003. pp. 457-474

[11] Burke E, Landa-Silva D, Soubeiga E. Multi-objective hyper-heuristic approaches for space allocation and timetabling. In: MIC 2003-Meta-Heuristics: Progress as Real Problem Solvers. USA: Springer; 2003. pp. 129-158

[12] McClymont K, Keedwell EC. Markov chain hyperheuristic (mchh): An online selective hyper-heuristic for multiobjective continuous problems. In: Proceedings of Genetic and Evolutionary Computation Conference (GECCO11); 2011. pp. 2003-2010

[13] Deb K, Jain S. Running performance metrics for evolutionary multiobjective optimization. Technical Report KanGAL Report No. 2002004. India: Kanpur Genetic Algorithms Laboratory, Indian Institute of Technology Kanpur; 2002

[14] Huband S, Hingston P, Barone L, While, L. A review of multiobjective test problems and a scalable test problem toolkit. IEEE Transactions on Evolutionary Computation. 2006;**10**:477-506

[15] McClymont K, Keedwell E, Savic, D. A general multi-objective hyper-heuristic for water distribution network design with discolouration risk. Journal of Hydroinformatics. 2013;**15**(3):700-716

[16] Rafique AF. Multiobjective hyper-heuristic scheme for system design and optimization. In: Proceedings of 9th International Conference on Mathematical Problems in Engineering, Aerospace and Science, AIP Conference 1493; 2012

[17] Kirkpatrick S, Gelatt C, Vecchi M. Optimization by simulated annealing. Science. 1983;**22**:671-680

[18] Kennedy J, Eberhart R, Shi Y. Swarm Intelligence. USA: Morgan Kaufmann; 2001

[19] Vázquez-Rodríguez J, Petrovic S. Calibrating continuous multi-objective heuristics using mixture experiments. The Journal of Heuristics. 2012;**18**:699-726

[20] Deb K, Controlled elitist nondominated sorting genetic algorithms for better convergence. In: Proceedings of Evolution Multi Criterion Optimization Conference; 2001. pp. 67-81

[21] Zitzler E, Künzli S. Indicator-based selection in multiobjective search. In: Lecture Notes in Computer Science, Parallel Problem Solving from Nature (PPSN VIII); USA: Springer; 2004. pp. 832-842

[22] Zitzler E, Laumanns M, Thiele L. Spea2: Improving the strength Pareto evolutionary algorithm for multiobjective optimization. In: EUROGEN 2001—Evolutionary Methods for Design, Optimization and Control with Applications to Industrial Problem. USA: Springer; 2001. pp. 95-100

[23] Kumari A, Srinivas K, Gupta M. Software module clustering using a hyperheuristic based multi-objective genetic algorithm. In: Advance Computing Conference (IACC), 2013 IEEE 3rd International; 2013. pp. 813-818

[24] Maashi, MS, Özcan E, Kendall G. A multi-objective hyper-heuristic based on choice function. Expert Systems with Applications. 2014;**41**(9):4475-4493

[25] Maashi MS, Kendall G, Özcan E. Choice function based hyper-heuristics for multi-objective optimization. Applied Soft Computing. 2015;**28**:312-326

[26] Maashi MS. An investigation of multi-objective hyper-heuristics for multi-objective optimisation [thesis]. Nottingham, UK: University of Nottingham; 2014

[27] Dueck G. New optimization heuristics: The great deluge algorithm and the record to record travel. Journal of Computational Physics. 1993;**104**:86-92

[28] Burke EK, Bykov Y. A late acceptance strategy in hill-climbing for exam timetabling problems. In: International Conference on the Practice and Theory of Automated Timetabling; 2008

[29] Fonseca C, Fleming P. Multiobjective optimization and multiple constraint handling with evolutionary algorithms. IEEE Transactions on Systems, Man, and Cybernetics. Part A: Systems and Humans. 1998;**28**(1):26-37

[30] Glover F. Future paths for integer programming and links to artificial intelligence. Computer Operations Research. 1986;13(5):533-549

[31] Liao X, Li Q, Yang X, Zhang W, Li W. Multiobjective optimization for crash safety design of vehicles using stepwise regression model. Structural and Multidisciplinary Optimization. 2008;**35**:561-569

[32] Li W, Özcan E, John R. Multi-objective evolutionary algorithms and hyper-heuristics for wind farm layout optimization. Renewable Energy. 2016;**105**:473-482

[33] Walker D, Keedwel, editors. Multi-objective optimisation with a sequence-based selection hyper-heuristic GECCO '16 companion. In: Proceedings of the 2016 on Genetic and

Evolutionary Computation Conference Companion; July 20-24, 2; Denver, Colorado, USA. New York, NY, USA: ACM; 2016. pp. 81-82

[34] Bai R, Woensel T, Kendall G, Burke EK. A new model and a hyper-heuristic approach for two-dimensional shelf space allocation. Journal Operation Research. 2013;**11**:31-55

[35] Veerapen N, Landa-Silva D, Gandibleux X. Hyperheuristic as component of a multi-objective metaheuristic. In: Proceedings of the Doctoral Symposium on Engineering Stochastic Local Search Algorithms (SLS-DS 2009); 2009

[36] Len C, Miranda G, Segura C. Hyperheuristics for a dynamic-mapped multiobjective island-based model. In: Distributed Computing, Artificial Intelligence, Bioinformatics, Soft Computing, and Ambient Assisted Living. In: Lecture Notes in Computer Science; Berlin Heidelberg: Springer; 2009. pp. 41-49

[37] Gomez J, Terashima-Marín H. Approximating multi-objective hyper-heuristics for solving 2D irregular cutting stock problems. In: Lecture Notes in Computer Science. In Advances in Soft Computing. USA: Springer; 2010. pp. 349-360

[38] Miranda G, Armas J, Segura C, León, C. Hyperheuristic codification for the multi-objective 2d guillotine strip packing problem. In: In Proceedings of IEEE Congress on Evolutionary Computation; 2010. pp. 1-8

[39] Armas J, Miranda G, and Leòn, C. Hyperheuristic encoding scheme for multiobjective guillotine cutting problems. In: In Proceedings of the 13th Annual Genetic and Evolutionary Computation Conference; 2011

[40] Furtuna R, Curteanu S, Leon F. Multi-objective optimization of a stacked neural network using an evolutionary hyper-heuristic. Applied Soft Computing. 2012;**12**(1): 133-144

[41] Vrugt J, Robinson B. Improved evolutionary optimization from genetically adaptive multimethod search. Proceedings of the National Academy of Sciences. 2007;**104**(3):708-711

[42] Haario H, Saksman E, Tamminen, J. An adaptive metropolis algorithm. Bernoulli. 2001;**7**:223-242

[43] Storn R, Price K. Differential evolution: A simple and efficient heuristic for global optimization over continuous. Journal of Global Optimization. 1997;(11):341-359

[44] Raad D, Sinkse A, Vuuren J. Multiobjective optimization for water distribution systemdesign using a hyperheuristic. Journal of Water Resources Management. 2010;**136**(5):592-596

[45] Zhang X, Srinivasan R, Liew MV. On the use of multi-algorithm, genetically adaptive multi-objective method for multi-site calibration of the swat model. Hydrological Processes. 2010;**24**(8):955-1094

[46] Wang Y, Li B. Multi-strategy ensemble evolutionary optimization for dynamic multiobjective optimization. Memetic Computing. 2010;**2**:3-24

[47] Deb K, Goldberg D. An investigation on niche and species formation in genetic function optimization. In: Proceedings of 3rd International Conference on Genetic Algorithms; 1989. pp. 42-50

[48] Bäck T. Evolutionary Algorithms in Theory and Practice. UK: Oxford University Press; 1996

[49] Deb K. Multi-Objective Optimization Using Evolutionary Algorithms. US: Wiley; 2001

[50] Anderson JM, Sayers TM, Bell MGH. Optimisation of a fuzzy logic traffic signal controller by a multiobjective genetic algorithm. IEEE Road Transport Information and Control. 2007;**454**:186-190

[51] Zhang Q, Li H. Evolutionary algorithms for multi-objective optimization: Performance assessments and comparisons. IEEE Transactions on Evolutionary Computation. 2007;**11**(6):712-731

[52] Li H, Zhang Q. Multiobjective optimization problems with complicated pareto sets, MOEA/D and NSGA-II. IEEE Transactions on Evolutionary Computation. 2009;**13**(2):284-302

[53] Li H, Landa-Silva D. An adaptive evolutionary multi-objective approach based on simulated annealing. Evolutionary Computation. 2011;**19**(4):561-595

[54] Auger A, Bader J, Brockhoff D, Zitzler E. Hypervolume-based multiobjective optimization: Theoretical foundations and practical implications. Theoretical Computer Science. 2012;**425**:75-103

[55] Bader J, Zitzler E. Hype: An algorithm for fast hypervolume-based many-objective optimization. Evolutionary Computation. 2008;**19**(1):45-76

[56] Sutton R, Barto A. Reinforcement Learning: An Introduction. USA: MIT Press; 1998

[57] Van Veldhuizen D. Multiobjective evolutionary algorithms: Classifications, analyses, and new innovations [thesis]. Wright-Patterson AFB. Ohio: Air Force Institute of Technology; 1999

[58] Glover F, Laguna M. Tabu search. In: Modern Heuristic Techniques for Combinatorial Problems. USA: John Wiley & Sons; 1995. pp. 70-150

[59] Kendall G, Mohamad M. Channel assignment in cellular communication using a great deluge hyperheuristic. In: IEEE International Conference on Network; 2004. pp. 769-773

[60] Zitzler E, Thiele L. Multiobjective evolutionary algorithms: A comparative case study and the strength Pareto approach. IEEE Transactions on Evolutionary Computation. 1999;**3**(4):253-290

[61] Srinivas N, Deb K. Multiobjective optimization using nondominated sorting in genetic algorithms. Evolutionary Computation. 1994;**2**(3):221-248

[62] Van Veldhuizen DA, Lamont G. Evolutionary computation and convergence to a pareto front. In: Proceedings of Late Breaking Papers at the Genetic Programming 1998 Conference; 1998. pp. 221-228

[63] Coello Coello CA, Cruz Cortés N. Solving multiobjective optimization problems using an artificial immune system. Genetic Programming and Evolvable Machines. 2005;**6**(2):163-190

Section 2

Scheduling Heuristics

Chapter 3

Heuristics Techniques for Scheduling Problems with Reducing Waiting Time Variance

Satyasundara Mahapatra, Rati Ranjan Dash and
Sateesh K. Pradhan

Additional information is available at the end of the chapter

http://dx.doi.org/10.5772/intechopen.69224

Abstract

In real computational world, scheduling is a decision making process. This is nothing but a systematic schedule through which a large numbers of tasks are assigned to the processors. Due to the resource limitation, creation of such schedule is a real challenge. This creates the interest of developing a qualitative scheduler for the processors. These processors are either single or parallel. One of the criteria for improving the efficiency of scheduler is waiting time variance (WTV). Minimizing the WTV of a task is a NP-hard problem. Achieving the quality of service (QoS) in a single or parallel processor by minimizing the WTV is a problem of task scheduling. To enhance the performance of a single or parallel processor, it is required to develop a stable and none overlap scheduler by minimizing WTV. An automated scheduler's performance is always measured by the attributes of QoS. One of the attributes of QoS is 'Timeliness'. First, this chapter presents the importance of heuristics with five heuristic-based solutions. Then applies these heuristics on $1||WTV$ minimization problem and three heuristics with a unique task distribution mechanism on $Q_m|prec|WTV$ minimization problem. The experimental result shows the performance of heuristic in the form of graph for consonant problems.

Keywords: task scheduling, quality of services, waiting time variance, single processor, uniform parallel processors

1. Introduction

In real world, scheduling is an approach through which a large number of tasks (jobs) are assigned to the resources (processors) that complete the task execution process in time. Due to the limitation of resources, a number of challenging issues are initiated on execution processes. Hence, huge numbers of tasks are waiting in a queue for execution. An efficient and convenient way of ordering between the tasks and resources is the only solution to resolve these issues. Such ordering is otherwise spelled as scheduling through which the efficiency and accuracy of the task execution process is enhanced. Designing and developing a stable and secured automated scheduler for real world problems is a real challenge for enhancing the quality of services (QoS) of the scheduler. A qualitative automated scheduler's performance is always measured by the attributes of QoS. One of the attributes of QoS is 'Timeliness', which measures the time taken to execute the task and produce an output.

Numerous criteria of timeliness provide good QoS to a task execution process. These criteria are response time, waiting time, turn-around time, elapsed time etc. Delay indicates the extra waiting time taken by the task due to the time consumed by the resources in an execution process. To optimize the scheduling process, new methods with objectives are adapted and integrated as per the requirements and constraints of the issues at hand. In case of discrete alternatives, scheduling is the discipline of decision making. Available resources, imposed constraints, and time required for executions are important factors to form a schedule. These factors are concern for an individual or a group. In real computational world, a series of activities to be outlined serially with the help of these factors is a challenge. This can be described as multiobjective optimization deterministic scheduling problem. The main objectives are to minimize the makespan and not to overlap two or more activities in the same time span with same resources.

Scheduling problems typically involve for search groupings, orderings, or assignments of a discrete set of activities, which satisfy the imposed conditions or constraints. These elements are generally modeled by means of countable discrete structures known as combinatorial structure. These structures are represented through a vector of decision variables which can assume values within a finite or a countable infinite set. Within these settings, a solution for a scheduling problem is a value assignment to the variables that meet specified criteria. Such cases formulate the scheduling problem exploiting the concepts of constraint satisfaction problems or optimization problems.

In Computer Science and Engineering, multiobjective optimization deterministic scheduling problems are belonging to a broad class of combinatorial optimization problems. These combinatorial optimization problems area belongs to NP hard, moreover asymptotically getting an optimal solution in linear time is impossible. In the field of Computer Science and Engineering, mathematical optimizations determine an optimal solution which may be an extremely time consuming procedure due to their computational complexity, whereas heuristic is a technique for finding an approximate solution. In other words, a heuristic is a procedure which produces a quick solution that is good enough for solving the problem at hand. This solution may not be the best of all the actual solutions to this problem, or it may simply approximate the exact solution. But it is still valuable because finding it does not require a prohibitively long time. This is achieved by trading optimality, completeness, accuracy, and precision for speed.

The rest of the section is structured as follows. A brief review of related work of different researchers in scheduling of tasks on single processor and parallel processor with motivation is mentioned in Section 2. In Section 3, the general definition of scheduling problem is briefly discussed. As scheduling is a NP-hard problem, different approaches for solving the scheduling problem are discussed in Section 4. The classification of deterministic scheduling problem is discussed briefly in Section 5. Different existing heuristic methods are discussed along with pseudo code in Section 6. The single processor scheduling problem with problem formulation and performance analysis of different heuristic methods is discussed in Section 7. In Section 8, the parallel processor scheduling problem with problem formulation and performance analysis of different heuristic methods is discussed. Section 9 contains a brief report on analysis of work leading to conclusion, scope for utilization of this study in different similar areas and suggestions for future research in this field.

2. Review of literature and motivation

In many manufacturing and services industries, scheduling is a decision making process that is used in a day-to-day basis. It deals with the allocation of resources to tasks over a given time period. In computational world, these resources are single processor, multi processors, parallel processors, and dedicated processors. The goal is to optimize one or more objectives such as makespan, mean flow time, mean weighted flow time, mean tardiness, mean earliness, etc. Scheduling problem is a broader class of combinatorial problem, and the purpose is to search a best way to organize task so that it is completed in the shortest possible time as depicted in Refs. [1, 2]. Importance of different types of real world scheduling problems such as single processor scheduling problem, two processor scheduling problems, parallel processor scheduling problems, job shop scheduling problems, flow shop scheduling problems, open shop scheduling problems, etc. are classified and discussed in Ref. [3] and play a significant role in research. The combinatorial problems are belonging to the real world problem. These problems are either problem of minimization or maximization. Such problems consist of a set of instances, candidate solutions for each instance, and a function that assigns to each instance and each candidate solution, a positive rational number called solution value is depicted in Ref. [4]. These problems are distinguished into three subclasses and presented in Ref. [5]. They are named as optimization problem, decision problem, and search problems. An optimization problem is defined as the answer to its instance that specifies a solution for which a value of a certain objective is at its optimum, whereas a decision problem takes only two values, either 'yes' or 'no', as an answer to the instance of the problem. Finally, the search problem simply aims at finding a valid solution, regardless of any quality criterion.

As scheduling is a decision making problem, effective algorithms are developed and designed by the researchers to solve it in due course of time. Such algorithms consist of two parts named as 'head' and 'method'. The head starts with the keyword 'algorithm' followed by a name (i.e., description for the purpose of algorithm), whereas method is used to describe the idea or logic used in the algorithm. The semantic representations are reflected with the help of layout of output, procedure or function name, variable, etc. These algorithms consist of a block of instructions used in a sequential order. Changing the instruction in algorithm changes the behavior of the algorithm is explained in Ref. [2].

Scheduling of task is an integral part of single and parallel computing. Extensive research has been conducted in this area leading to significant theoretical and practical results. New scheduling algorithms are in demand for addressing concerns originating from the single and parallel processors. How heuristic methodology encourages the researcher to explore and pursue the creative journey through internal discovery in the field of research is presented in Ref. [6].Two heuristic task scheduling methods for single processor, called balanced spiral (BS) and verified spiral (VS), which incorporate certain proven properties of optimal task sequences for minimizing the waiting time variance is proposed in Ref. [7]. The success of stochastic algorithms is often due to their ability to effectively amplify the performance of search heuristics that is focused and discussed in Ref. [8]. A heuristic procedure to minimize the weighted completion time variance in single processor is presented in Ref. [9]. Two heuristic methods named as EC1 an EC2 are developed and proposed in Ref. [10] for solving the problem for a set of large tasks by minimizing waiting time variance in the single machine problem. A novel heuristic method named as RSS is developed and proposed in Ref. [11] for solving the problem for large set of tasks by minimizing waiting time variance in the single machine problem.

Several meta-heuristics have been inspired by nature in due course of time. Two well-known robust metaheuristic methods, including genetic algorithm (GA), simulated annealing (SA), were improved and presented in Ref. [12] to tackle large-scale problems. A MAX-MIN Ant System, which makes use of a separate local search routine, is proposed in Ref. [13] for tackling a typical university course timetabling problem. An ant algorithm based on a multiagent system inspired by the observation of some real ant colony behavior exploiting the stigmergic communication paradigm is discussed in Ref. [14]. An agent-based parallel genetic algorithm for job shop scheduling problem is proposed in Ref. [15]. A genetic algorithm (GA) has been developed in Ref. [16] for minimizing the average residence time to produce a set of batches in function of batch order in a multipurpose-multiproduct batch plant. Multi objective genetic algorithm to find a balance point in respect of a solution of the Pareto front is presented in Ref. [17]. A decomposition heuristics algorithm based on multibottleneck processors for large-scale job shop scheduling problems is proposed in Ref. [18]. A new heuristic based on adaptive memory programming and a simulated annealing algorithm is presented in Ref. [19].

To enhance the property of different heuristic methods for parallel processing in uniform processors, a unique task allocation scheme named as PUM is developed and presented in Ref. [20]. One exact algorithm and one approximation algorithm are proposed in Ref. [21] to minimize the completion time variance. A heuristic algorithm to solve preemptive scheduling problem of dependent tasks on parallel identical processors is proposed in Ref. [22]. A new heuristic algorithm for scheduling metatasks in heterogeneous computing system is presented in Ref. [23]. Heuristic algorithms are proposed to solve a number of independent tasks on multiple number of identical parallel processors problem so as to minimize the waiting time variance [24].

In computing systems, while working with large data files on a Web server, often the response time to a user's request is strongly dependent on the time required to access or retrieve the data files referenced by the user. Especially in online systems, it is often desirable to provide uniform response to user's requests, i.e., minimize the variance of response time by minimizing the variance of access time. The variance of completion time and variance of waiting time performance measures are analyzed [25] for the single processor sequencing problem. These measures are compared and contrasted to the performance measures of mean completion time and mean waiting time. It was shown that the sequence that minimizes the variance of waiting times is antithetical to the sequence that minimizes the variance of flow times, which motivate to take waiting time variance as the performance parameter.

Another motivation is to find out the effectiveness of the methods used for calculation of WTV in parallel processor by efficient task allocation scheme, which will be able to generate a schedule with less time as far as possible.

3. Scheduling problems

The deterministic scheduling problems are part of a much broader class of combinatorial optimization problems. To analyze these problems, the peculiarities of the problem must be studied. The time required for solving those scheduling problems is seriously limited, so that only low-order polynomial time algorithms may be used. Thus, the examination of the complexity of these problems should be the basis for analysis of scheduling problems and algorithms, which is shown in **Figure 1** as a problem solving cycle for deterministic scheduling problem.

The deterministic scheduling problems can be defined as a combination of a set of tasks '$\mathcal{T}$', a set of processors '$\mathcal{P}$', and a set of additional resources '$\mathcal{R}$'. Scheduling means to assign processors from $\mathcal{P}$ and possibly, resources from $\mathcal{R}$ to tasks from $\mathcal{T}$ in order to complete all tasks under the imposed constraints. There are two general constraints arise in classical scheduling theory. They are, each task is to be processed by at most one processor at a time, and each processor is capable of processing at most one task at a time. The processors may be either parallel (i.e., performing the same functions) or dedicated (i.e., specialized for the execution of certain tasks). The parallel processors are distinguished as identical, uniform, and unrelated

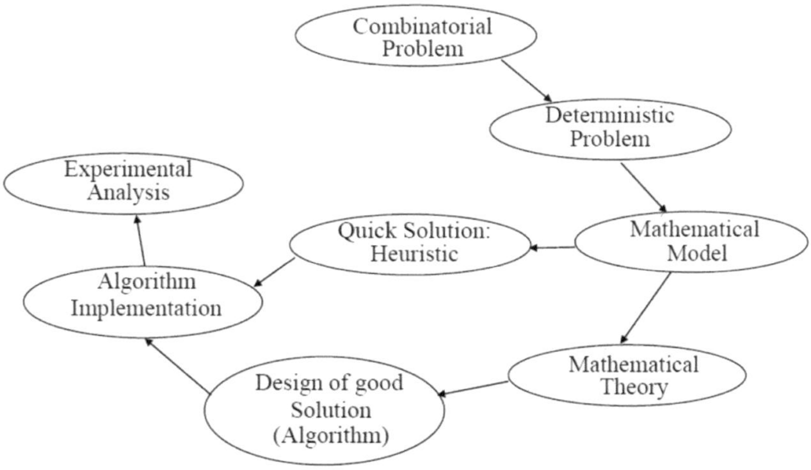

Figure 1. Problem solving cycle for deterministic scheduling problem.

depending on their speeds. In identical, all processors have equal task processing speeds. Similarly, the uniform processors have different speed and unrelated processors depend on the particular task.

The dedicated processors are distinguished as task shop, flow shop, and open shop. In task shop, each task has its own predetermined route to follow with a set of processors. But a distinction is made between task shops in which each task visits each processor at most once and task shops in which a task may visit each processor more than once. On the contrary in flow shop, a set of processor are placed in series. Each task has to be processed on every processor exactly once. All tasks have to follow the same route, i.e., they have to be processed first on processor 1, then on processor 2, and so on. In case of open shop, a set of tasks must be processed for given amounts of time at each of a given set of processors, in an arbitrary order. The idea is to determine the time at which each task is to be processed at each processor. In such systems, it is assumed that the buffers between processors have unlimited capacity and a task after completion on one processor may wait before its processing starts on the next one. However, buffers of zero capacity tasks cannot wait between two consecutive processors are termed as no-wait property.

The classical deterministic scheduling problem can be stated as follows. There are a set of n tasks simultaneously available for being processed on a set of m processors. Let all tasks available for processing at time zero. Each task j, $j \in \mathcal{T} = \{1, 2, \ldots, n\}$, passes through the processors 1, 2, ..., m in that order and requires an uninterrupted processing time pt_{ij} on processor i, $i \in \mathcal{P} = \{1, 2, \ldots, m\}$. The scheduling objective is to minimize makespan. Makespan or maximum completion time is the time interval between starting the first task on a processor and the completion of the last processor and denoted by C_{max}. Let $\mathcal{T}_j$ be the set of subtasks scheduled on processor i. Then, the completion time on processor i can be computed as $C_i = \Sigma_{j \in \mathcal{P}_i} pt_{ij}$. Hence, maximum completion time, i.e., makespan can be calculated as $C_{max} = max_{i \in \mathcal{P}} C_i$. To minimize the makespan of a deterministic scheduling problem, apriori knowledge on different procedure of scheduling schemes is required and discussed in the next section.

4. Approaches to scheduling problems

From the literature review, it was observed that there exists a large class of combinatorial optimization problems for which most probably no polynomial optimization algorithms are available. These are the problems whose decision counterparts are NP complete. Hence, in such cases, the optimization problems are NP hard. A comprehensive study on NP completeness, NP hardness, polynomial time transformation, etc. helps the researchers in analyzing the multiobjective scheduling problem. It also helps the researchers to solve those problems by using polynomial time algorithm. The usefulness of the algorithm depends on the order of its worst-case complexity function and on the particular application. It was found that sometimes, the worst-case complexity function is not low enough, although still polynomial, a mean complexity function of the algorithm may be sufficient. On the other hand, if the decision version of the analyzed problem is NP complete, then there are several approaches taken into consideration to make the problem NP hard. These approaches are discussed below.

First, constraints like allowing preemptions, assuming unit-length tasks, and assuming certain types of precedence graphs are relaxed by imposing on the original problem and then solving the relaxed problem. The solution of the latter may be a good approximation to the solution of the original problem. In case of computer application, the relaxation method is justified when parallel processors share a common primary memory. Moreover, such a relaxation is also advantageous from the viewpoint of certain optimality criteria.

Second, in the process of solving NP hard scheduling problems, the use of approximation algorithms tends to find an optimal schedule but does not always succeed. It is a useful heuristic for finding near optimal solutions, when the optimal solution is not required [5]. The necessary condition for these algorithms to be applicable in practice is that their worst-case complexity function is bounded from above by a low-order polynomial in the input length. So that approximation algorithm often give raise to heuristic that return solution much closer to optimal than indicated by their performance guarantee and bring the researchers to study of heuristics and allowed to prove how well the heuristic performs on all instances [5]. Their sufficiency follows from an evaluation of the difference between the value of a solution they produce and the value of an optimal solution. This evaluation may concern the worst case or a mean behavior. However, for some combinatorial problems, it can be proved that there is no hope of finding an approximation algorithm of certain accuracy.

Analysis of the worst-case behavior of an approximation algorithm may be complimented by an analysis of its mean behavior. This can be done in two ways. The first consists in assuming that the parameters of instances of the considered problem are drawn from a certain distribution, and then the mean performance of algorithm is analyzed. Distinguish between the absolute error and the relative error asymptotic optimality results in the stronger (absolute) sense are quite rare. On the other hand, asymptotic optimality in the relative sense is often easier to establish. It is rather obvious that the mean performance can be much better than the worst-case behavior, thus justifying the use of a given approximation algorithm. A main obstacle is the difficulty of proofs of the mean performance for realistic distribution functions. Thus, the second way of evaluating the mean behavior of approximation algorithms, consisting of experimental studies, is still used very often in real world problems.

The third and the last way of dealing with hard scheduling problems is to use exact enumerative algorithms whose worst-case complexity function is exponential in the input length. Such problems are not NP hard in strong sense. These problems are possible to solve by pseudo-polynomial optimization algorithm whose worst-case complexity function is bounded from above by a polynomial in the input length and in the maximum number appearing in the instance of the problem. For reasonably small numbers, such an algorithm may behave quite well in practice, and it can be used even in computer applications.

The above discussion is summarized in a schematic way in **Figure 2**. It is observed that finding an exact algorithm for a large-scale task scheduling problem is not easy. Hence, local optimum

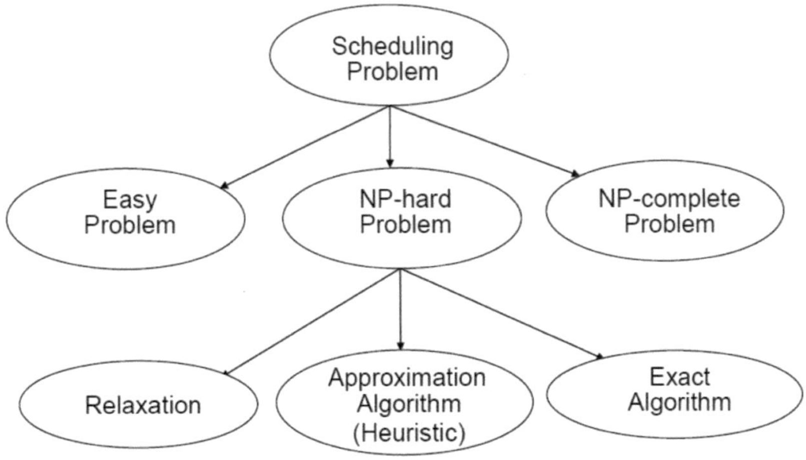

Figure 2. Approaches to scheduling problem.

algorithm as heuristic is always better to develop and to be used. Knowledge of classification for these scheduling problems serves as a basis for developing heuristic algorithms, which is discussed in next session.

5. Classification of deterministic scheduling problems

A scheduling problem is described by a triplet $(\alpha | \beta | \gamma)$ and shows the possible classification under the each parameter of the triplet [26]. A detailed nature of triplet is explained in appendix A. The symbol α is represented for processor environment and contains only one entry that is classified into two types, named as single processor and multiple processors. Single processor again is classified into three categories. They are named as single processor, parallel processor, and dedicated processor.

Parallel processors are classified as per their behavior of the parallelisms into three types. They are named as identical parallel processors, uniform parallel processors, and unrelated parallel processors denoted by the symbol P, Q, and R, respectively. Similarly dedicated processors are classified into three categories named as flow shop processors, task shop processors, and open shop processors denoted by the symbol F, J, and O, respectively.

The symbol β is represented for different types of tasks and resource constraints. It may contain no entry at all, a single entry, or multiple entries. The possible entries in the β field are preemption (*pmtn*) used for the interruption of task and re-start in latter, resource (*res*) used for identification of particular type of resource, precedence (*prec*) required for the completion of one or more tasks before another task is allowed to start its processing, ready time (r_j) represents the task j starting time for processing, delivery time (q_j) represents the time spent for delivery the task j after its processing, processing time (pt_j) represents the processing time of task j on a processor, deadline ($\tilde{d}$) are imposed on the performance of a task set, maximal number of tasks ($n_j \leq k$) describes the maximal number of sub-tasks (n_j) constituting a task (k) in

Completion time	C_j
Flow time	$F_j = C_j - r_j$
Lateness	$L_j = C_j - d_j$
Tardiness	$D_j = max\{C_j - d_j, 0\}$
Earliness	$E_j = max\{d_j - C_j, 0\}$
Tardy task unit	$U_j = \begin{cases} 1 & if\ C_j > d_j \\ 0 & Othewise \end{cases}$

Table 1. Objective functions.

case of task shop systems, and no-wait ($no - wait$) describes a no-wait property in the case of scheduling on dedicated processors.

The symbol γ is represented as objective function for minimizing the different performance measure (i.e., optimality criteria) of scheduling and contains single entry only. These measures are depicted in Ref. [26], and the parameter required for computing these objective function of a task j is calculated and given in **Table 1**.

As it has been observed from different research articles that a good number of objectives are available for minimizing the different performance measure of scheduling, the ultimate objective is minimizing the makespan. To fulfill the aforementioned objective under different constraints, several methods have been developed which therefore gives raise to various classes of schedules.

6. Heuristic methods for scheduling problems

From the literatures, it is observed that a number of task ordering methods are developed and improved in due course of time. These methods either belong to exact or heuristic or meta-heuristic methods. In the process of searching a best or improved method with desired objective, all possible solutions are tested one by one. This process is viable only for small size of problems but very challenging, complicated, and time consuming as the size of problem increases. Therefore, to reorder the tasks of large problems, heuristic methods are developed for obtaining optimum solution. The solutions obtained by the heuristic methods are optimum or near optimum in nature by using less number of computer resources and computational time. Calculation of CTV and WTV are the two objectives for these types of heuristics. For minimizing the WTV, Elion & Chowdhary, verified spiral (VS), balanced spiral (BS), and Rati-Satya-Sateesh (RSS) heuristic methods are discussed below.

6.1. Eilon and Chowdhary (EC1 & EC2)

EC1 and EC2 are two types of heuristics, designed and presented in Ref. [10] for an n-task WTV problem. Here, 'n' numbers of tasks are scheduled on the basis of V shape property of optimal sequence. In case of EC1, the largest processing time task is removed from the job queue and placed at last position of the schedule. The second largest processing time task is removed from the job queue and placed at the first position of the schedule. Similarly, the third largest processing time task is removed from the job queue and placed at the last but one position of the schedule. The fourth largest processing time task is removed from the job queue and placed in second position of the schedule. This process continues until the job queue is empty. This method places the jobs in a spiral front and rear manner. EC2 heuristic, the modified version of EC1, produces the task schedule by incorporating the Schrage's conjecture with EC1. The Schrage's conjecture states that there exists an optimal sequence in which the largest job is scheduled at last position, the second longest is at first position, the third and fourth longest are last-but-one position and last-but-two position, respectively, in the sequence [27].

6.2. Verified spiral (VS)

Verified spiral (VS) presented in Ref. [7] is an improved version of EC1. This method incorporates Schrage's conjecture and Hall & Kubiak's proof [28] about the placement of first three largest processing time tasks. For the remaining task on the task queue, a modified spiral placement method is implemented. This method removes the next task from the task queue and place either after the front task or before the rear task of the sequence on the basis of which position produces a small WTV with the existing tasks.

6.3. Balanced spiral (BS)

The balanced spiral (BS) method discussed in Ref. [7] is developed to reduce the computational cost of VS method. This method is otherwise known as observation method, as it balance the left (L) and right (R) optimal sequence to get optimum or near optimum sequence after placing the processing time of each tasks in sequence one by one until the task queue is empty.

6.4. Rati-Satya-Sateesh (RSS)

In our locality, the fishmongers are those who sell a whole unit of fish. Sometimes a large fish has to be distributed equally to two or more customers. These fishmongers are so skilled that they can equally distribute the cut pieces of the same fish among the customers during the time of cutting. It reduces the post measurement for equality, which generally found almost equal. This distribution mechanism to serve the customers used in this method is named as RSS, presented in Ref. [20]. This method allocates the tasks in the sequence with minimum computational cost and time.

The effectiveness of the above discussed methods is presented in the next two sections by using single processor and parallel processors with an objective WTV.

7. Single processor scheduling

In the task scheduling problem, '*n*' number of tasks has to be processed by a single processor with some processing objectives, order, and constraints. Discovering an optimized schedule, which minimizes the WTV of the tasks, is the aspiration of the problem. Due to nonavailability of the processor in real time, a task has to wait for processing, as the processor is processing another task and may also due to the precedence process constraint.

In the process of searching, an effective and optimized sequence of tasks, it needs to calculate all possible combination of tasks (factorial n). It consumes much time and resources to give an optimum sequence. Different heuristics and meta-heuristics methods are required to develop by reducing the number of calculations for handling many concurrent tasks in computer and in network systems. To achieve this service stability on an individual recourse, it is required to minimize the WTV, which is the objective of the task scheduling problem on single processor.

7.1. Problem formulation

The above mentioned problem can typically describe as an allocation of tasks to a processor by considering the concept that once a task get into the processor for processing, it did not leave from the processor until the processing time of that task was over. The decision whether the task "j" (i.e., the task number) is scheduled to the processor successfully, then "k" the allocation variable is 1 (one) or 0 (zero) otherwise, which can be represented by an integer. These decision variable depends upon the position of task in the task sequence, which is represented by s_{kj} for $k \in \mathcal{L} = \{1, 2, \ldots, n\}$ and $j \in \mathcal{T} = \{1, 2, \ldots, n\}$. The task to be scheduled first is placed at first position, thus processed first; the task to be scheduled second is placed at second position, thus processed second, and so on. Then, the waiting time for task j at position k is represented as wt_{kj} and the processing time of task j is represented by pt_j. The WTV of tasks in a complete sequence is obtained as follows in Eq. (S.1).

$$WTV = \frac{1}{n-1}\sum\nolimits_{j \in \mathcal{L}_k}\left(wt_{kj} - \frac{1}{n}\sum\nolimits_{j \in \mathcal{L}_k} wt_{kj}\right)^2 \tag{S.1}$$

The objective is to minimize the variance of waiting time of n number of tasks can be found by Eq. (S.2).

$$Minimize\ 1||WTV \tag{S.2}$$

subject to:

$$\sum\nolimits_{k \in \mathcal{T}_j} s_{kj} = 1 \tag{S.3}$$

$$\sum\nolimits_{j \in \mathcal{L}_k} s_{kj} = 1 \tag{S.4}$$

$$s_{kj} = 0\ or\ 1 \quad \forall k \in \mathcal{L},\ j \in \mathcal{T} \tag{S.5}$$

$$wt_{kj} = 0 \quad \forall k = 1\ ,\ j \in \mathcal{T} \tag{S.6}$$

$$wt_{kj} \geq wt_{k-1\,j} + \sum\nolimits_{j \in \mathcal{L}_k} s_{k-1\,j} * pt_j \quad \forall k \in \mathcal{L}\ ,\ j \in \mathcal{T} \tag{S.7}$$

The constraint that each position of the sequence is used exactly once by a task is described in Eq. (S.3). Each task is assigned to a position in the sequence is exactly described once in

Eq. (S.4). The integer constraint for decision variable is described in Eq. (S.5). The waiting time for the first task is described in Eq. (S.6), and the waiting time wt_{kj} of the task at position k ($k >= 2$) is described in recursive Eq. (S.7).

7.2. Problems for testing and performance analysis

This section presents the effectiveness of five heuristic algorithms discussed in section 6 by generating the test cases with the help of three probability distributions namely normal distribution, Poisson distribution, and exponential distribution. At first, a small set of test cases have been selected which are same as used in Refs. [7, 10] to find the effectiveness of the algorithms. To increase the number of testing cases, another three large sets of data are also generated randomly of 5 through 500 numbers of tasks. These large data sets are generated with the help of normal, Poisson, and exponential distribution, respectively.

To measure the performance of the heuristics presented in Section 6, at first for optimality, all possible sequences are generated by placing the tasks randomly for each problem of small data set. Each generated possible sequence is considered as one sub example of all possible optimal sequences. For example, there are 120 numbers of task sequences (e.g., 5!) are generated for 5 numbers of tasks. Similarly, there are 720 numbers of task sequences (e.g., 6!) are generated as there are six tasks so on. But the above discussed five heuristic methods generate only one task sequence for each test case of small data set. The basic aim is to calculate WTV for the test cases, which satisfy the V-shaped optimal property.

Figure 3 shows the WTV performance of five heuristic methods is as good as the performance of optimal methods for small size test cases. It was also observed that the RSS method gives optimum or near optimum WTV results as compared with optimum generated WTV value.

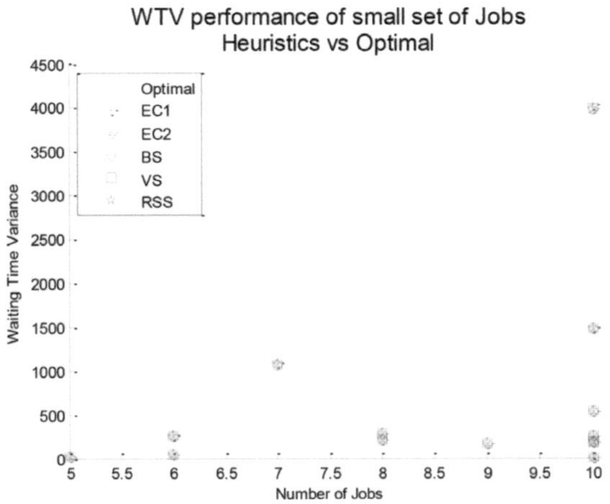

Figure 3. WTV performance of between heuristics vs optimal for small set of jobs.

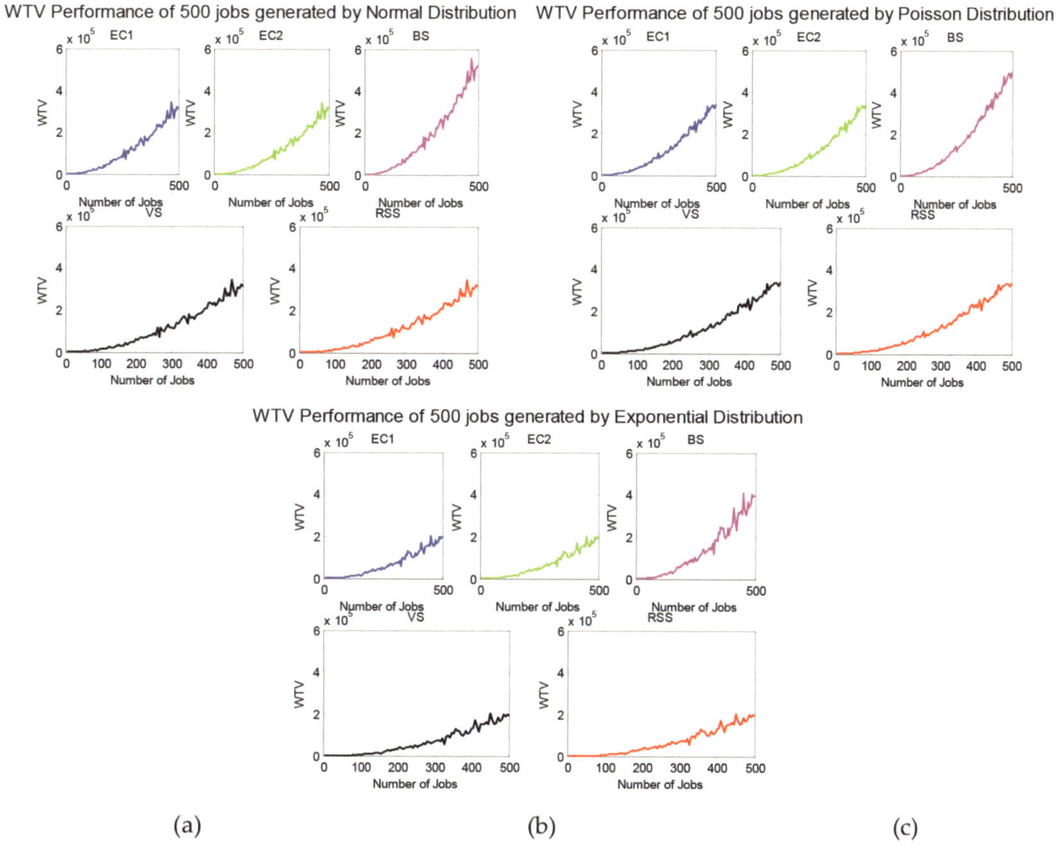

Figure 4. Performance of WTV with respect to heuristics methods for large set of data (i.e., processing time) generated by normal, Poisson, and exponential distribution.

The WTV performance of EC1, EC2, VS, BS, and RSS heuristic methods for all the test cases of large data set is shown in **Figure 4**. The computational result depicted that the WTV obtained by RSS method seems to be near optimum in comparison with other four methods for different numbers of tasks generated by three distribution methods discussed above.

For single processor scheduling problem, the computational cost is treated as computational average time. It is observed that all heuristic methods used sorting mechanism before the generation of tasks sequence except optimal method. Quick sort is an efficient sorting mechanism that takes *O (n log n)* computational cost. It is also observed that the sequence generated by VS method takes much larger computational cost than BS and RSS method as the calculation of WTV is made multiple times. The sequence generated by BS method also takes larger computational cost than RSS method as the calculation of total processing time is made multiple times. Hence, by applying the concept of cutting a large fish into small pieces and distributed among the customers uniformly by a fishmonger generate an optimum or near optimum sequence by minimizing WTV in very less computational cost is a major achievement.

8. Parallel processor scheduling

Parallel processing is one of the arising concepts that used to schedule a batch of *'n'* numbers of tasks to be processed by *'m'* numbers of parallel processors [24]. This section presents a parallel scheduling algorithm as a solution to the problem $Q_m | prec | WTV$ with an effect of minimization of mean WVT. This approach is a heuristic based and the tasks are allocated dynamically in the task sequence by keeping variance as a controlling parameter. The tasks are placed in the individual sequence with the help of heuristic algorithms, so that the dynamic heuristic methods take extremely less computational cost. These algorithms are tested on randomly generated problems of varying numbers of tasks and processors as parameters. The effectiveness with respect to mean WTV is done by comparing the result among the discussed heuristic methods. The findings are shown in graphic form for corresponding problems.

8.1. Problem formulation for task scheduling problem

The uniform parallel processors $i \in \mathcal{P} = \{1, 2, \ldots, m\}$ are having different speeds $s \in \mathcal{S} = \{1, 2, \ldots, m\}$ with the relation $s_1 < s_2 < s_3 < \ldots < s_m$. This means that the first processor is the slowest processor with low processing cost and the last processor is the fastest processor with high processing cost. For a given task, the processing times on the uniform parallel processor is in the ratios listed as $1/s_1 : 1/s_2 : 1/s_3 : \ldots : 1/s_m$. The processors are continuously available, and they are never kept idle while work is waiting. The processors are assigned by the maximum processing time capacity of a task, so that allotments of tasks are assigned on the basis of the processing time. Thus, low processing time tasks are assigned to slowest processors and highest processing time tasks are assigned to fastest processors. The designed uniform scheduling problem is based on the allocation of n, numbers of independent tasks $j \in \mathcal{T} = \{1, 2, \ldots, n\}$ as per the processing time at location $k \in \mathcal{L} = \{1, 2, \ldots, n\}$ on a set of m numbers of uniform parallel processors $i \in \mathcal{P} = \{1, 2, \ldots, m\}$.

The problem is formulated under five numbers of assumptions. At first, the starting time of individual processors are assumed to initialize at time 0 (zero). In other words, all the tasks for each processor are ready to begin for processing at the same time, i.e., 0 (zero). Second, each processor is available deliberately prior to a condition that once the processor given a task to process, it cannot be preempted until the task's processing time is completed on that processor. Third, once a task is allocated to any one processor, it cannot be laid away to other processor under any circumstance. Fourth, the number of tasks must be greater than the number of processors, i.e., $n > m$, as the problem with $n \leq m$ is irrelevant. Fifth, all the allocated processors will be waiting according to the order of allocation, i.e., after the previously allocated task has been finished the present task can be started.

From the literature, it was observed that number dominant properties on WTV problem has been discovered and depicted by the researchers. To start, first for any scheduling sequence R, *CTV* of R is equal to *WTV* of R', where R' is the antithetical schedule of R [25]. Second, the scheduling sequence that minimizes *WTV* is antithetical to the scheduling sequence that minimizes *CTV* [25]. Third, *CTV* remains unchanged when reversing the order of the last $n1$ tasks [25]. Fourth, for *CTV* minimization problems, an optimal scheduling sequence is of the form of (n, $n-2$, ..., $n-1$), i.e., the largest task is arranged at the first position, the second longest task is arranged at the last position, and the third longest task is arranged at the second position [28]. Fifth, the optimal sequence for a WTV minimization problem is V shaped [10]. Sixth, $P_m \| CTV$ problem is NP complete in the strong sense when 'm' is arbitrary [24]. Seventh, $P_m \| CTV$ Problem is NP complete in the ordinary sense when 'm' is fixed [24].

Minimization of WTV as a performance measure for task scheduling problem has been discussed in Section 7 for achieving the service stability between the tasks in single processor. The parallel processor is nothing but multiple numbers of single processors with same speed or multiple numbers of single processors with different speed are working simultaneously for achieving the concurrency. Hence, to come up with an optimized schedule, which minimize the WTV is the aspiration of the task scheduling problem in parallel environment. The WTV developed (S.1) in Section 7 will be utilized for the development of the WTV on parallel processors. The WTV of tasks in a complete sequence for the parallel processor is obtained as follows in Eq. (P.1).

$$WTV = \frac{1}{m}\sum_{i \in \mathcal{P}}\left(\frac{1}{n_i - 1}\sum_{j \in \mathcal{L}_{ki}}\left(wt_{kij} - \frac{1}{n_i}\sum_{j \in \mathcal{L}_k} wt_{kij}\right)^2\right) \tag{P.1}$$

The objective is to find an optimum or near optimum schedule with pseudo-polynomial time of $Q_m | prec | WTV$ problem by minimizing the variance of waiting time for n number of tasks on m number of uniform parallel processors by Eq. (P.2).

$$Minimize\ (Q_m|prec|WTV) \tag{P.2}$$

subject to:

$$\Sigma_{j \in \mathcal{P}i}\, s_{kij} = 1 \quad \forall\, k \in \mathcal{L} \tag{P.3}$$

$$\Sigma_{i \in \mathcal{T}_j} s_{kij} = 1 \quad \forall\, k \in \mathcal{L} \tag{P.4}$$

$$\Sigma_{j \in \mathcal{P}_i} wt_{kij} = 0 \quad \forall\, k = 1 \tag{P.5}$$

$$wt_{kij} = wt_{k-1ij} + \Sigma_{j \in \mathcal{P}_i} s_{kij} * pt_j \quad \forall\, k \in \mathcal{L},\ j \in \mathcal{T},\ i \in \mathcal{P} \tag{P.6}$$

$$\Sigma_{j \in \mathcal{P}_i} q_{kij} = 1\ \forall\, k \in \mathcal{L} \tag{P.7}$$

$$q_{kij} * N + wt_{k+1ij} \geq wt_{kij} + \Sigma_{j \in \mathcal{P}_i} s_{kij} * pt_j \quad \forall\, k \in \mathcal{L},\ j \in \mathcal{T},\ i \in \mathcal{P} \tag{P.8}$$

$$s_{kij} \in \{0, 1\} \quad \forall\, k \in \mathcal{L},\ j \in \mathcal{T},\ i \in \mathcal{P} \tag{P.9}$$

$$q_{kij} \in \{0, 1\} \quad \forall\, k \in \mathcal{L},\ j \in \mathcal{T},\ i \in \mathcal{P} \tag{P.10}$$

$$C_{kij} \geq 0 \quad \forall\, k \in \mathcal{L},\ j \in \mathcal{T},\ i \in \mathcal{P} \tag{P.11}$$

$$wt_{kij} \geq 0 \quad \forall\, k \in \mathcal{L},\ j \in \mathcal{T},\ i \in \mathcal{P} \tag{P.12}$$

where N is large number.

Each task is assigned to a position is exactly once in any one of the processor sequence is described in Eq. (P.3). Each position of any one process or sequence is used exactly once by a task is described in Eq. (P.4). The waiting time for first task of the individual processor sequence is described in Eq. (P.5). The waiting time of all other allotted tasks for the individual processor except first one is described in Eq. (P.6). Eqs. (P.7) and (P.8) state that if two tasks are on the same processor, then one must be scheduled after the other; otherwise, the values of wt_{kij} and wt_{k+1ij} will not be related. Eqs. (P.9) and (P.10) indicate that the introduced decision variables are binary in nature. Eqs. (P.11) and (P.12) represent that the value of completion time and waiting time must be greater than zero.

8.2. Task allocation methods for uniform parallel processors

The uniform parallel processors are identified by their different speeds. The processors are arranged in chronological order, such that the first processor is the slowest processor with low processing cost and the last processor is the fastest processor with high processing cost. The scheduling problem ($Q_m | prec | WTV$) discussed above is a combinatorial problem. Therefore, usage of a heuristic is inevitable to obtain solution in polynomial time. The challenge is to distribute the tasks in an efficient manner among the processors. A unique task allocation method named as PUM is presented in Ref. [20] for the allocation of tasks among the processors.

Uniform parallel processors consist of a bank of single processors with different speed, and the computational cost is depending on the speed of the processors. It is most important to allocate the task in such a way that the computational cost must be maintained. Hence, the unique task allocation scheme named as PUM is combined with the heuristic methods namely VS, BS, and RSS is also discussed in Ref. [20]. The efficiency of the three heuristic methods with the unique task allocation scheme for uniform parallel processors is tested with a large number of test cases discussed in the next section.

8.3. Problems for testing and performance analysis

To find the effectiveness of these heuristic methods, test cases are randomly generated with the help of four probability distributions. At first with the help of normal distribution, 901 numbers of test cases are generated randomly in combination of 5 and 6 numbers of uniform parallel processors for each case of 100 through 1000 numbers of tasks. The test cases are followed by the same number of tasks and processors with the help of Poisson distribution, exponential distribution, and uniform distribution. The performance analysis of the heuristic methods with unique task allocation scheme is discussed below.

For analysis, mean WTV is taken as the measure of performance. Performance of measure of three heuristic methods named as VS, BS, and RSS is analyzed by using a unique task allocation scheme named as PUM. This enhances the performance of heuristic methods for parallel processing in uniform processors. The allocation scheme in combination with heuristic algorithms is tested with a large number of test cases starting from 100 to 1000 tasks separately. The results analysis for normal distribution on uniform parallel processor is presented in **Figure 5**,

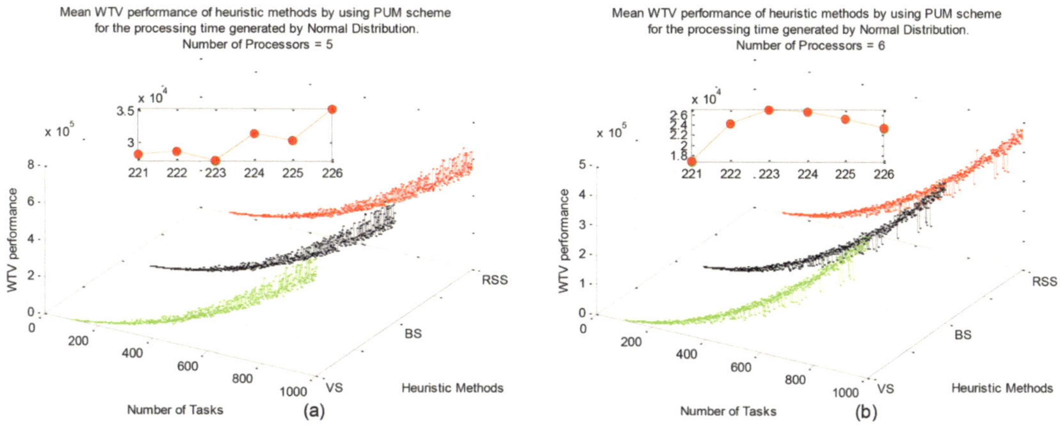

Figure 5. Comparison of mean WTV with respect to heuristics methods by using PUM allocation scheme for the processing time generated by normal distribution.

which consists of two subfigures (a) and (b). The mean WTV obtained by the three heuristic algorithms with the help of unique task allocation scheme is shown in each subfigure. The task allocation schemes are implemented on each test case generated by normal distributions. The subfigures (a) and (b) represent mean WTV performance for 5 and 6 numbers of uniform parallel processors, respectively. The three heuristic methods are represented in each subfigure (a) and (b) by three distinct colors. Green color represents VS method, black color represents BS method, and red color represents RSS method. An enlarged view of mean WTV performance of heuristic methods from total task numbers 221 to 226 is presented in each subfigure. The computational result shows that the mean WTV obtained by RSS methods in combination of PUM is apparently same in comparison with other two heuristic methods.

Similarly, the processing time for all the test cases is generated with the help of Poisson, exponential, and uniform distribution, respectively. It is also observed that mean WTV obtained by RSS methods in combination of PUM are apparently same in comparison with other two heuristic methods as presented in Ref. [20].

Developing an efficient task allocation scheme and execute it with the heuristic methods for uniform parallel processors is NP hard. To overcome it in uniform parallel processor, an efficient task allocation scheme is required along with the heuristic methods. The average time required for finding sequence by computing the heuristics in uniform parallel processor is represented as computational cost. From the above discussed heuristic methods with PUM allocation scheme, it is found that the VS method requires at least four tasks to commence, and all the heuristic methods discussed in Section 6 need a sorting procedure after the PUM allocation process is over and before the starting of heuristic process. Quick sort is an efficient sorting mechanism that takes $O(n \log n)$ computational cost. Hence, it is used to sort the tasks before implementation of heuristics. From the performance analysis, it is observed that the computational cost of VS method is much larger then BS and RSS method, as the calculation of WTV is made multiple times, and the computational cost of BS method is also larger than the

RSS method, as the calculation of total processing time is made multiple times. It is therefore revealed that the computational cost of RSS method is the least.

9. Conclusion and future scope

This work is motivated from the various criteria of timeliness that provide services to the users of computer and network systems including response time, waiting time, turn-around time, elapsed time etc. To provide uniform response to the users, i.e., to minimize the variance of response time by minimizing the variance of access time is the problem of task scheduling by minimizing WTV as a measure in single processor and extend to parallel processors. In other words, a step has been taken for developing a scheduling procedure that minimizes the WTV of the individual task.

In task scheduling problems, a lot of works are done on the area of completion time rather than waiting time. Variance as a parameter is introduced by the researcher to minimize the CTV by distributing the task processing time in such a way that the uniformity among the task is obtained (i.e., QoS). For obtaining the uniformity in the scheduling problems, variance of completion time is more effective rather than the completion time. It was also found that the sequence that minimizes the variance of completion time is antithetical to the sequence that minimizes the variance of waiting time. But it was found from the literature that a large number of works are done on CTV, and in case of WTV, it is few.

The aim of this work is to analyze, study the peculiarity behavior, and develop efficient heuristic methods for solving different classes of scheduling problems. As the addressed problems are NP hard, the alternative of using heuristic methods has been proven to be good one, whereas the exact solution always gives optimum solution by taking maximum time for both single processor as well as parallel processors for a large set of tasks.

In these respects at first, basic elements of classical deterministic scheduling problem, different aspects related to scheduling problem and algorithms, and classification of scheduling problems are presented. Second, different methods for solving scheduling problems, complexity of scheduling problem, and basic knowledge on different schedule class are discussed. At last, an overview on different objective classification criteria for both single processor and parallel processors was presented.

Using the aforementioned background, a mixed integer programming model with two scheduling problems was addressed:

- A single processor scheduling problem *Minimize* $(1||WTV)$ for minimizing WTV was stated and solved in section 7 by using five heuristic methods namely as EC1, EC2, VS, BS, and RSS.
- The processing time of tasks are generated randomly by three probability distributions namely normal distribution, Poisson distribution, and exponential distribution.
- Performances of five heuristic methods are analyzed. It was observed that RSS method gives optimum or near optimum results than other heuristic methods

- From the comparative result, it was also observed that the obtained WTV of the sequence generated with the help of heuristic methods are always satisfying the V-shaped optimality property.
- It was also observed that RSS method gives results with minimum computational cost than other heuristic methods.
- A uniform parallel processor scheduling problem *Minimize* ($Q_m | prec | WTV$) for minimizing WTV was proposed and solved in Section 8 by using a RSS method in combination with a unique proposed task allocation scheme named as PUM.
- A unique task allocation scheme was developed for allocating the task to individual processor.
- The processing time of tasks are generated randomly by four probability distributions namely normal distribution, Poisson distribution, exponential distribution, and uniform distribution.
- Performance of measure of three heuristic methods namely as VS, BS, and RSS are analyzed by using a unique task allocation scheme named as PUM.
- The experimental results are compared and observed that RSS method with PUM allocation scheme reveals the best solution with minimal computational cost.

Therefore, it is concluded that in case of single processor, the computational cost of RSS heuristic method is less than the other four heuristic methods. In case of uniform parallel processor, the RSS method with PUM allocation scheme reveals the optimum or near optimum solution with minimal computational cost.

Often new computer systems and new performance measures used to evaluate a system lead to new directions in scheduling. The environment of scheduling is changing time to time depending on resource availability, interruptions, and nature of changed demand. New scheduling is to be prepared in between an old unprocessed schedule. This give rise to change in constraints and resources. This has to be rescheduled with changed objectives.

In future, keeping WTV as the measure of performance the following works will be carried out for finding the suitability and effectiveness of the heuristic methods and task allocation schemes proposed in this work.

- To apply the proposed work for available multiobjective scheduling problems.
- To apply the proposed work in order to investigate the field of tasks and resources allocation in project like project management scheduling, broadcast scheduling, etc.
- To find out the effect of these proposed work in dynamic scheduling.
- Exploration of more efficient scheduler with better effective scheduling methods.
- Use of stochastic scheduling problems in real life environment.
- Suitability of techniques with cloud computing which is a kind of grid with virtual services and service oriented architecture (SOA).

Author details

Satyasundara Mahapatra[1]*, Rati Ranjan Dash[2] and Sateesh K. Pradhan[3]

*Address all correspondence to: satyasundara123@gmail.com

1 Indian Institute of Science and Information Technology, Bhubaneswar, India

2 College of Engineering and Technology, Bhubaneswar, India

3 Utkal University, Bhubaneswar, India

References

[1] Graham RL. Combinatorial scheduling theory. In: Steen LA, editors. Mathematics Today. Vol. 3. Berlin: Springer; 1978. pp. 183–211.

[2] Graham RL. The combinatorial mathematics of scheduling. Scientific American. 1978;**238**: 124–132.

[3] Katona GOH. Combinatorial search problems. In: Srivastava JN, editors. A Survey of Combinatorial Theory. Vol. 28. Amsterdam: North-Holland Publ. Co; 1973.

[4] Garey MR, Johnson DS. Computers and Intractability, A Guide to the Theory of NP-Completeness. New York, USA: W.H. Freeman and Company; 2000.

[5] Williamson DP, Shmoys DB. The Design of Approximation Algorithm. Vol. 3. Cambridge, UK: Cambridge University Press; 2010.

[6] Djuraskovic I, Arthur N. Heuristic inquiry: A personal journey of acculturation and identity reconstruction. The Qualitative Report. 2010;**1**(6): 1569–1593.

[7] Nong Ye, Li X, Farley T, Xu X. Job scheduling methods for reducing waiting time variance. Computer & Operations Research (Elsevier). 2007;**18**:3069–3083.

[8] Vincent AC, Stephen F Smith. Heuristic Selection for Stochastic Search Optimization: Modeling Solution Quality by Extreme Value Theory. 10th International Conference, CP, Toronto, Canada, Proceedings, Vol. 3. 2004. pp. 197–211.

[9] Nessah R, Chu C. A lower bound for weighted completion time variance. European Journal of Operational Research. 2010;**10**(3):1221–1226.

[10] Eilon S, Chowdhury IG. Minimizing waiting time variance in the single machine problem. Management Science. 1977;**34**(6):567–575.

[11] Mahapatra S, Dash RR, Pradhan SK. An approach to solve single machine job scheduling problem using heuristic algorithm. International Journal of Emerging Technologies in Computational and Applied Sciences (IJETCAS), ISSN (Online): 2279-0055. 2015;**11**(2):157–163.

[12] Poursalik K, Miri-Nargesi S. Meta-heuristic approaches for a new modeling of single machine scheduling problem. Scientific Khyber. 2013;**55**(2):107–117.

[13] Socha K, Knowles J, Sampels M. A MAX-MIN ant system for the university timetabling problem. In: Dorigo M, Di Caro G, Sampels M (editors). Ant Algorithms: Third International Workshop, ANTS 2002. Lecture Notes in Computer Science. Vol. 16; 2002. pp.1–13.

[14] Dorigo M, Bonabeau E, Theraulaz G. Ant algorithms and stigmergy. Future Generation Computer. 2000;**16**(8):851–871.

[15] Asadzadeh L, Zamanifar K. An agent-based parallel approach for the job shop scheduling problem with genetic algorithms. Mathematical and Computer Modelling. 2010;**52** (11–12): 1957–1965.

[16] Baudet P,Azzaro C, Pibouleau L, Domenech S. A genetic algorithm for batch chemical plant scheduling. Proc. Int. Congress of Chemical and Process Engineering. 1996:pp. 25–30.

[17] Cardon A, Galinho T, Vacher JP. A multi-objective genetic algorithm in job shop scheduling problem to refine an agents architecture. In Proceedings of EUROGEN'99. Jyvaskyla, Finland. University of Jyvsaskyla; 1999.

[18] Zhai Y, Liu C, Chu W, Guo R, Liu C. A decomposition heuristics based on multi-bottleneck machines for large-scale job shop scheduling problems. Journal of Industrial Engineering and Management (JIEM). 2014;**177**(5):1397–1414.

[19] El-Bouri A, Azizi A, Zolfaghari S. A comparative study of a new heuristic based on adaptive memory programming and simulated annealing: The case of job shop scheduling. European Journal of Operational Research. 2007;**155**:1894–1910.

[20] Mahapatra S, Dash RR, Pradhan SK. A heuristic for scheduling of uniform parallel processors. 2nd International Conference on Computational Intelligence and Networks (CINE), KIIT University, Bhubaneswar, Odisha. IEEE Xplore Digital Library. 11 Jan 2016:78–83.

[21] Cai X, Cheng TCE. Multi-machine scheduling with variance minimization. Discrete Applied Mathematics. 1998;**128**(1–3):55–70.

[22] Jozefowska J, Mika M, Rozycki R, Waligora G, Weglarz J. An almost optimal heuristic for preemptive C_{max} scheduling of dependent tasks on identical parallel processors. Annals of Operation Research. 2004;**129**(129):205–216.

[23] Rafsanjani MK, Bardsiri AK. A new heuristic approach for scheduling independent tasks on heterogeneous computing systems. International Journal of Machine Learning and Computing. 2011;**2**(4):371–376.

[24] Xu X, Ye N. Minimization of job waiting time variance on identical parallel machines. IEEE transactions on Systems, Man, and Cybernetics–Part C: Applications and Reviews. 2007;**37**(5):917–927.

[25] Merten AG, Muller ME. Variance minimization in single machine sequencing problems. Management Science. 1972;**38**(9):518–528.

[26] Pinedo M. Scheduling theory, algorithms and systems. Englewood Cliffs, NJ: Prentice-Hall; 1995.

[27] Schrage L. Minimizing the time-in-system variance for a finite jobset. Management Science. 1975;**207**(5):540–543.

[28] Hall NG, Kubiak W. Proof of a conjecture of Schrage about the completion time variance problem. Operations Research Letters. 1991;**27**:467–472.

Chapter 4

Efficient Heuristics for Scheduling with Release and Delivery Times

Nodari Vakhania

Additional information is available at the end of the chapter

http://dx.doi.org/10.5772/intechopen.69223

Abstract

In this chapter, we describe efficient heuristics for scheduling jobs with release and delivery times with the objective to minimize the maximum job completion time. These heuristics are essentially based on a commonly used scheduling theory in Jackson's extended heuristic. We present basic structural properties of the solutions delivered by Jackson's heuristic and then illustrate how one can exploit them to build efficient heuristics.

Keywords: combinatorial optimization, heuristic algorithm, scheduling theory, time complexity, approximation algorithm

1. Introduction

The *combinatorial optimization* problems have emerged in late 40s of last century due to a rapid growth of the industry and new arisen demands in efficient solution methods. Modeled in mathematical language, a combinatorial optimization problem has a finite set of the so-called *feasible solutions*; this set is determined by a set of restrictions that naturally arise in practice. Usually, there is an objective function in which domain is the latter set. One aims to determine a feasible solution that gives an extremal (minimal or maximal) value to the objective function, the so-called *optimal solution*. Since the number of feasible solutions is typically finite, theoretically, finding an optimal solution is trivial: just enumerate all the feasible solutions calculating for each of them the value of the objective function and select any one with the optimal objective value. The main issue here is that a brutal enumeration of all feasible solutions might be impossible in practice.

There are two distinct classes of combinatorial optimization problems, class P of polynomially solvable ones and NP-hard problems. For a problem from class P, there exists an efficient (polynomial in the *size* of the problem) algorithm. But no such algorithm exists for an *NP*-hard problem. The number of feasible solutions of an *NP*-hard optimization problem grows exponentially with the size of the input (which, informally, is the amount of the computer memory necessary to represent the problem data/parameters). Furthermore, all *NP*-hard problems have a similar *computational* (*time*) *complexity*, in the sense that if there will be found an efficient polynomial-time algorithm for any of them, such an algorithm would yield another polynomial-time algorithm for any other *NP*-hard problem. On the positive side, all *NP*-hard problems belong to the *class NP* that guarantees that any feasible schedule to an *NP*-hard problem can be found in polynomial time. It is believed that it is very unlikely that an *NP*-hard problem can be solved in polynomial time (whereas an exact polynomial-time algorithm with a reasonable real-time behavior exists for a problem in class *P*). Hence, it is natural to think of an approximation solution method.

Thus, approximation algorithms are most frequently used for the solution of *NP*-hard problems. Any *NP*-hard problem has a nice characteristic, that is, any feasible solution can be created and verified in polynomial time, like for problems in class *P*. A *greedy* algorithm creates in this way a single feasible solution by iteratively taking the next "most promising" decision, until a complete solution is created. These decisions are normally taken in a low-degree polynomial/constant time. Since the total number of iterations equals to the number of objects in a given problem instance, the overall time complexity of a greedy algorithm is low. Likewise, *heuristic* algorithms reduce the search space creating one or more feasible solutions in polynomial time. Greedy and heuristic algorithms are simplest approximation algorithms. It is easy to construct such an algorithm for both polynomial and *NP*-hard problems. It may deliver an optimal solution to a problem from calls *P*, but it is highly unlikely that a heuristic optimal algorithm may exist for an *NP*-hard problem. A greedy algorithm reduces the potential search space by taking a unique decision for the extension of the current partial solution in each of the n iterations. A simplest heuristic algorithm is greedy, though there are more sophisticated heuristic algorithms that use different search strategies. In general, an approximation algorithm may guarantee some worst-case behavior measured by its *performance ratio*: the ratio of the value of objective function of the worst solution that may deliver the algorithm to the optimal objective value (a real number greater than 1).

Scheduling problems are important combinatorial optimization problems. A given set of requests called *jobs* are to be performed (scheduled) on a finite set of resources called *machines* (or *processors*). The objective is to determine the processing order of jobs on machines in order to minimize or maximize a given objective function. Scheduling problems have a wide range of applications from production process to computer systems optimization.

Simple greedy heuristics that use some priority dispatching rules for the for taking the decisions can be easily constructed and adopted for scheduling problems. An obvious advantage of such heuristics is their rapidness, and an obvious disadvantage is a poor solution quality. The generation of a better solution needs more computational and algorithmic efforts. A *Global search* in the feasible solution space guarantees an optimal solution, but it can take inadmissible computational time. A *local* (*neighborhood*) *search* takes reasonable computational time, and the solution which it gives is locally best (i.e., best among all considered neighbor solutions).

Simulated annealing, tabu-search, genetic algorithms, and beam search are examples of local search algorithms (for example, [16, 22, 23, 25]). These algorithms reduce the search space, and at the same time, their search is less restricted than that of simple heuristic (dispatching) algorithms, giving, in general, better quality solutions than simple greedy algorithms. Global search methods include (exact) implicit enumerative algorithms and also approximative algorithm with embedded heuristic rules and strategies (for example, [1, 20, 29, 38, 4]). Normally, global search algorithms provide the solutions with the better quality than the local search algorithms, but they also take more computer time.

This chapter deals with one of the most widely used greedy heuristics in scheduling theory. The generic heuristic for scheduling jobs with release and delivery times on a single machine to minimize the maximum job completion time is named after Jackson [21] (the heuristic was originally proposed for the version without release times, and then it was extended for the problem with release times by Schrage [30]). Jackson's heuristic (J-heuristic, for short), iteratively, at each scheduling time t (given by job release or completion time), among the jobs released by time t schedules one with the largest delivery time. This 2-approximation heuristic is important on its own right, and it also provides a firm basis for more complex heuristic algorithms that solve optimally various scheduling problems that cannot be solved by a greedy method.

In this chapter, we give a brief overview of heuristic algorithms that are essentially based on J-heuristic. Then, we go into the analysis of the schedules created by J-heuristic (J-schedule), showing their beneficial structural properties. They are helpful for a closer study of the related problems, which, in turn, may lead to better solution methods. We illustrate how the deduced structural properties can be beneficially used by building an adaptive heuristic algorithm for our generic scheduling problem with a more flexible worst-case performance ratio than that of J-heuristic.

The next section consists of four subsections. In Section 2, we first describe our basic scheduling problem, Jackson's heuristic, other related heuristics, and real-life applications of the scheduling problem. In Section 3, we study the basic structural properties of the schedules constructed by Jackson's heuristic. In Section 4, we derive a flexible worst-case performance estimation for the heuristic, and in Section 5, we construct a new adaptive heuristic based on Jackson's heuristic. Section 6 concludes the chapter with final remarks.

2. Preliminaries

2.1. Problem formulation

Our generic single-machine scheduling problem can be described as follows. We have n jobs from set J and a single machine. Job $j \in J$ is characterized by its *release time* r_j, a time moment when it becomes available. Once a released job is assigned to the machine, it takes p_j time units of uninterrupted processing time on that machine. Here, we have a basic restriction that the machine can process no more than one job at any time moment. Once job j completes its processing on the machine, it still needs a (constant) *delivery time* q_j for its *full completion* (the jobs are delivered by an independent unit and this takes no machine time). We wish to minimize the maximum job full completion time.

The problem is known to be strongly *NP* hard (Garey and Johnson [13]). According to the conventional three-field notation introduced by Graham et al. [18], the above problem is abbreviated as $1|r_j,q_j|C_{\max}$: in the first field, the single-machine environment is indicated, the second field specifies job parameters, and the third field specifies objective criteria.

The problem has an equivalent formulation $1|r_j|L_{\max}$ in which delivery times are interchanged by *due dates* and the maximum job *lateness* $L_{\max}$, that is, the difference between the job completion time and its due date is minimized (due date d_j of job j is the desirable time for the completion of job j).

We may note that, besides job lateness, there are other due-date-oriented objective criteria. A common one is *the number of late* jobs, where job is late if it completes behind its due date. Here, the number of late jobs is to be minimized. In the *feasibility* version of the problem, one looks for a schedule with no late job. Obviously, if in an optimal solution of the minimization version, the maximum job lateness is no more than 0, then it is a feasible solution of the feasibility version as well; otherwise (the maximum job lateness is positive), there exists no feasible solution to the feasibility version. Vice versa, an algorithm for the feasibility problem can be used to solve the minimization version: we iteratively increase due dates of all jobs until we find a feasible schedule with the modified due dates. Note that the min-max job lateness obtained in this way depends on the maximum job processing time $p_{\max}$ and n so that we will need to apply a feasibility algorithm $O(np_{\max})$ times. But by using binary search, the cost can be reduced to $O(log(np_{\max}))$.

Given an instance of $1|r_j,q_j|C_{\max}$, one can obtain an equivalent instance of $1|r_j|L_{\max}$ as follows. Take a suitably large constant K (no less than the maximum job delivery time) and define due date of every job j as $d_j = K - q_j$. Vice versa, given an instance of $1|r_j|L_{\max}$, we may create an equivalent instance of $1|r_j,q_j|C_{\max}$ by introducing job delivery times, $q_j = D - d_j$, taking a suitably large constant D (any number larger than the maximum job due date would work). It can be easily seen by the equivalence of these instances (if the makespan for the version $1|r_j,q_j|C_{\max}$ is minimized, the maximum job lateness in $1|r_j|L_{\max}$ is minimized, and vice versa, see Bratley et al. [2] for more details). Because of the equivalence, both above formulations might be used interchangeably.

2.2. Description of J-heuristic

Now, we describe Jackson's greedy heuristic (J-heuristic) in detail that works on n scheduling times (at every scheduling time, the next job is scheduled on the machine). Initially, the earliest scheduling time is set to the minimum job release time. Iteratively, among all jobs released by a given scheduling time, a job with the maximum delivery time is scheduled on the machine (ties might be broken by selecting any longest available job). Once a job completes on the machine, the next scheduling time is set to the maximum between the completion time of that job and the minimum release time of a yet unscheduled job.

Since the heuristic always schedules an earliest released job every time, the machine becomes idle and it creates no gap that can be avoided. The time complexity of the heuristic is $O(n \log n)$ as at every n scheduling times, the search for a maximal element in an ordered list is carried out.

The heuristic is easily expendable for multiprocessor and preemptive scheduling problems with release and delivery (due) times. For m identical parallel processor case, a ready job with the largest tail (or smallest due date) is repeatedly determined and is scheduled on the processor with the minimal completion time ties being broken by selecting the processor with the minimal index. For the sake of conciseness, we below refer to that processor as the *active* one.

Multiprocessor J-heuristic

$U := J;\ t := \min\{r_j | j \in U\}$

while $U \neq \emptyset$ **do**

begin

find job $j^* \in \{j \in U | r_j \leq t\}$ with the largest delivery time q_{j^*} and schedule it at time t on the corresponding active processor; $U := U \setminus \{j^*\}$;

update the current active processor and set t to the maximum between the completion time of that processor and minimal job release time in set U

end

We illustrate a 3-processor J-schedule in **Figure 1** for eight jobs with the parameters as specified in the table as follows:

$r_1 = 0$	$p_1 = 4$	$q_1 = 30$
$r_2 = 0$	$p_2 = 5$	$q_2 = 25$
$r_3 = 5$	$p_3 = 3$	$q_3 = 20$
$r_4 = 8$	$p_4 = 6$	$q_4 = 15$
$r_5 = 8$	$p_5 = 10$	$q_5 = 22$
$r_6 = 15$	$p_6 = 2$	$q_6 = 5$
$r_7 = 20$	$p_7 = 4$	$q_7 = 30$
$r_8 = 25$	$p_8 = 7$	$q_8 = 10$

As it can be seen in **Figure 1**, J-heuristic creates idle time intervals (the gaps) on all three processors constructing an optimal schedule with makespan 54. Note that job 7 realizes the maximum objective value 54 being scheduled on processor 2 (we call such job the overflow job

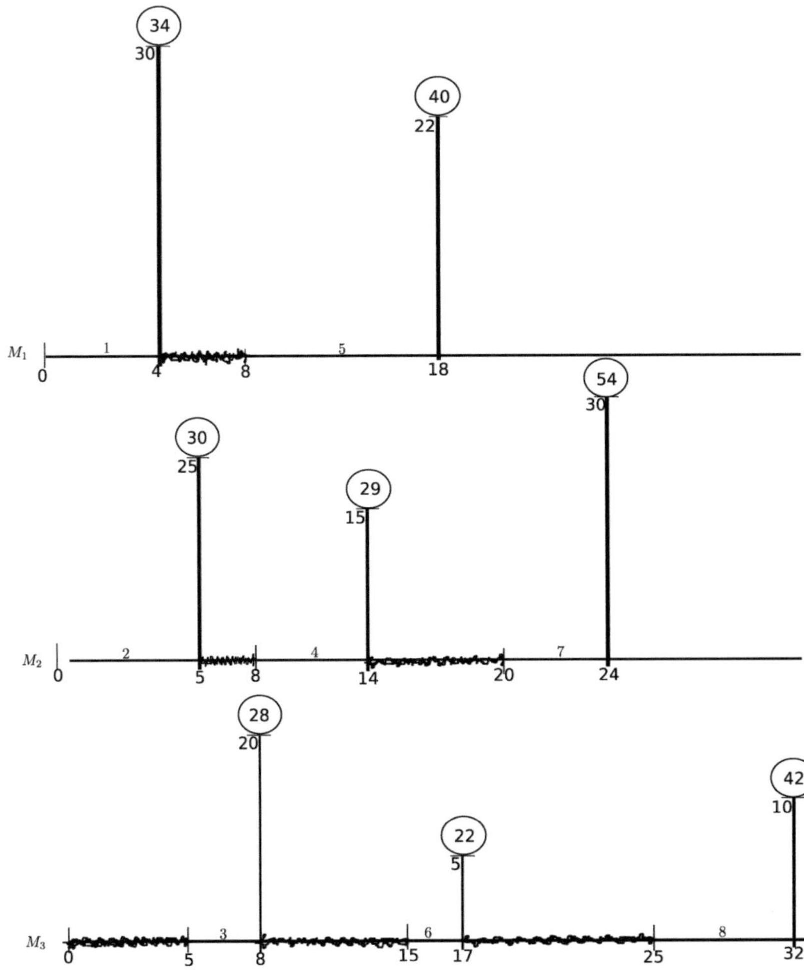

Figure 1. A 3-processor J-schedule. Zig-zag lines represent gaps, and the numbers within the circles are job full completion times.

as we define a bit later), the completion time of processor 2 is 24 (that of job 7), whereas the full completion time of job 7 is 54.

For preemptive version of J-heuristic, every currently executed job is interrupted at the earliest time moment when a more urgent jobs get released. It is well-known and also easily seen that the preemptive version of J-heuristic delivers an optimal solution for the corresponding preemptive scheduling problem.

2.3. Overview of related heuristics

As mentioned earlier, J-heuristic turned out to be highly flexible in the sense that its different modifications have been used for the solution of different scheduling problems. Potts [27] has proposed an extension of the heuristic. His algorithm repeatedly applies J-heuristic $O(n)$ times and obtains an improved approximation ratio of 3/2 at the cost of an increase by a factor of $O(n)$ time complexity. Hall and Shmoys [19], also based on J-heuristic, have developed another 4/3-approximation polynomial-time algorithm with the same time complexity of $O(n^2 \log n)$ for the version of our problem $1|r_j,q_j|C_{\max}$ with precedence relations. Garey et al. [14] have modified the heuristic as another more sophisticated $O(n \log n)$ heuristic for the feasibility version of this problem with equal-length jobs (in the feasibility version, job due dates are replaced by deadlines and a schedule in which all jobs complete by their deadlines is looked for). This result was extended to the version of problem $1|r_j,q_j|C_{\max}$ with two possible job processing times in an $O(n^2 \log n)$ algorithm described in [34]. For another relevant criterion, an $O(n^3 \log n)$ algorithm that minimizes the number of late jobs with release times on a single machine when job preemptions are allowed was proposed in [35]. Without preemptions, an $O(n^2 \log n)$ algorithm for the case when all jobs have equal length was proposed in [37].

Multiprocessor version of J-heuristic has been used as a basis for the solution of multiprocessor scheduling problems. For example, for the feasibility version with m identical machines and equal-length jobs, algorithms with the time complexities $O(n^3 \log \log n)$ and $O(n^2 m)$ were proposed in Simons [31] and Simons and Warmuth [32], respectively. Using the J-heuristic as a schedule generator, an $O(q_{\max} mn \ \log n + O(mvn))$ algorithm for the minimization version of the latter problem was proposed in [33], where $q_{\max}$ is the maximum job delivery time and $v < n$ is a parameter. With the objective to minimize the number of late jobs on a group of identical processors, an $O(n^3 \log n \log p_{\max})$ non-preemptive algorithm for equal-length jobs was proposed in [36].

J-heuristic can be efficiently used for the solution of shop scheduling problems. Using J-heuristic as a schedule generator, McMahon and Florian [24] and Carlier [5] have proposed efficient enumerative algorithms for $1|r_j,q_j|C_{\max}$. Grabowski et al. [17] use the heuristic for the obtainment of an initial solution in another enumerative algorithm for the same problem.

The problem $1|r_j,q_j|C_{\max}$ naturally arises in job-shop scheduling problems as an auxiliary problem for the derivation of strong lower bounds. By ignoring the potential yet unresolved conflicts on all the machines except a selected machine M, the corresponding disjunctive graph defines an auxiliary instance of problem $1|r_j,q_j|C_{\max}$ on machine M, where every task o to be performed on that machine is characterized by an early starting time (defined by the early completion times of its predecessor-tasks) that is set as its release time r_o and the tail or the delivery time q_o (determined by the processing times of the predecessor-tasks of task o). In multiprocessor job-shop scheduling problems, a single machine is replaced by a group of parallel machines, and the corresponding multiprocessor version of problem $1|r_j,q_j|C_{\max}$ is derived. For the purpose of a lower bound, preemptive version of the above problems with release and delivery times might be considered and preemptive J-heuristic can then be applied. For relevant studies on a classical job-shop scheduling problem, see, for example, Carlier [5], Carlier and Pinson [6], Brinkkotter and Brucker [3], and more recent works of Gharbi and Labidi [15] and Della Croce and T'kindt [12] and for multiprocessor job-shop scheduling problem with identical machines, see Carlier and Pinson [7]. This approach can also be extended for the case when parallel machines are unrelated [38].

J-heuristic can also be useful for parallelizing the computations in scheduling job shop [26] and also for the parallel batch scheduling problems with release times [10].

2.4. Some other applications

Besides the above-mentioned applications in multiprocessor, shop, and batch scheduling problems, our problem has numerous immediate real-life applications in various production chains, CPU time sharing in operating systems (jobs being the processes to be executed by the processor), wireless sensor network transmission range distribution (where jobs are mobile devices with their corresponding ranges that can be modeled as release and due dates), and important transportation problems such as traveling salesman's and vehicle routing problems with time windows. The reader may wish to have a look at reference [28] for an extensive overview of the variations of the vehicle routing problem, and we also refer to [11, 41] for more recent related work.

Our scheduling problem can be used for the solution of the latter transportation problems. Let us first describe these problems briefly. There are, say, n customers or cities and one special location called depot. The distances between any pair of locations are known. The goods are to be distributed from depot to the customers using one or more (identical) vehicles. There are certain restrictions on how this distribution should be done that define set of all feasible solutions to the problem. A general notion is a tour carried out by a vehicle that initiates at depot, visits some of the customers, and returns to depot. All customers must be served, i.e., every customer is to be included in exactly one tour. There may be additional restrictions such as vehicle capacity constraints and customer requests. And another basic constraint, which relates these transportation problems with our scheduling problem, is that every customer can be served only within a certain time interval, whereas there is also a valid time interval given for the depot.

A common objective is to minimize the total service/travel time of all the vehicles. Whereas in the basic setting, it is straightforward to find a feasible solution, with time windows, this task is not obvious, in fact, there may exist no feasible solution. If it exists, then one aims to minimize the number of used vehicles and then construct the corresponding number of tours with the objective to minimize total service time.

Associating with every customer and the depot a unique job and with the corresponding time window the release and due dates of that job, we arrive at a corresponding scheduling problem, an instance of $1|r_j|L_{\max}$. Let us consider the feasibility version of this problem (in which a solution with no positive lateness is looked for). Note that if there is no feasible solution to that feasibility version, then there exists no feasible solution to the corresponding vehicle routing problem with a single vehicle. Then, we may consider the feasibility problem with two identical machines $P2|r_j|L_{\max}$ and so on, with k identical machines $Pk|r_j|L_{\max}$, until a feasible solution is found. We may use a binary search within the interval $[1, m]$ instead when an upper limit m on the maximum number of vehicles is known (otherwise, we set m to a sufficiently large magnitude). In case, there exists a feasible solution for $k = m$, once the minimum k is found, the corresponding k tours minimizing the total travel time might be constructed.

3. The structure of J-schedules

Previous section's brief survey clearly indicates importance of our scheduling problem and the power and flexibility of J-heuristic as well. Whenever the direct application of J-heuristic for the solution of the problem is concerned and the solution quality is important, the worst-case bound of two may not be acceptable. Besides, J-heuristic may not solve the feasibility version of our problem even though there may exist a feasible solution with no positive maximum lateness. To this end, there are two relevant points that deserve mentioning. On the one hand, the practical behavior of the heuristic might be essentially better than this worst-case estimation [40]. On the other hand, by carrying out structural analysis of J-schedules, it is possible to obtain a better, more flexible worst-case bound, as we show in the next section. In this section, we introduce some basic concepts that will help us in this analysis.

Let us denote by σ, the schedule obtained by the application of J-heuristic to the originally given problem instance (as we will see later, this heuristic can also be beneficially applied to some other derived problem instances). Schedule σ, and, in general, any J-schedule, may contain a *gap*, which is its maximal consecutive time interval in which the machine is idle. We shall assume that there occurs a 0-length gap (c_j, t_i), whenever job i starts at its earliest possible starting time (that is, its release time) immediately after the completion of job j; here, t_j (c_j, respectively) denotes the starting (completion, respectively) time of job j.

Let us call a *block*, a maximal consecutive part of a J-schedule, is consisting of the successively scheduled jobs without any gap in between (preceded and succeeded by a gap).

Now, we give some necessary concepts from [33] that will help us to expose useful structural properties of the J-schedules.

Given a J-schedule S, let i be a job that realizes the maximum job lateness in S, i.e., $L_i(S) = \max_j\{L_j(S)\}$. Let, further, B be the block in S that contains job i. Among all the jobs in B with this property, the latest scheduled one is called an *overflow job* in S (we just note that not necessarily this job ends block B).

A *kernel* in S is a maximal (consecutive) job sequence ending with an overflow job o such that no job from this sequence has a due date more than d_o. For a kernel K, we let $r(K) = \min_{i\in K}\{r_i\}$.

It follows that every kernel is contained in some block in S, and the number of kernels in S equals to the number of the overflow jobs in it. Furthermore, since any kernel belongs to a single block, it may contain no gap.

If schedule σ is not optimal, there must exist a job less urgent than o, scheduled before all jobs of kernel K that delays jobs in K (see Lemma 1 a bit later). By rescheduling such a job to a later time moment, the jobs in kernel K can be restarted earlier. We need some extra definitions to define this operation formally.

Suppose job i precedes job j in ED-schedule S. We will say that *i pushes j* in S if ED-heuristic will reschedule job j earlier whenever i is forced to be scheduled behind j.

Since the earliest scheduled job of kernel K does not start at its release time (see Lemma 1 below), it is immediately preceded and pushed by a job l with $d_l > d_o$. In general, we may have more than one such a job scheduled before kernel K in block B (one containing K). We call such a job an *emerging job* for K, and we call the latest scheduled one (job l above) the *live* emerging job.

Now, we can give some optimality conditions for J-schedules. The proofs of Lemmas 1 and 2 can be found in references [33, 39], respectively. Lemma 4 is obtained as a consequence of Lemmas 1 and 2, though the worst-case bound of two was also known earlier.

Lemma 1. *The maximum job lateness (the makespan) of a kernel K cannot be reduced if the earliest scheduled job in K starts at time $r(K)$. Hence, if a J-schedule S contains a kernel with this property, it is optimal.*

From Lemma 1, we obtain the following corollary:

Corollary 1. *If schedule σ contains a kernel with no live emerging job ($E(\sigma) = \varnothing$), then σ is optimal.*

Observe that the conditions of the Lemma 1 and Corollary 1 are satisfied for our first problem instance of **Figure 1**. We also illustrate the above-introduced definitions on a (1-processor) problem instance of $1|r_j,q_j|C_{\max}$ with 11 jobs, job 1 with $p_1 = 100$, $r_1 = 0$, and $q_1 = 0$. All the rest of the jobs are released at time moment 10, have the equal processing time 1, and the delivery time 100. These data completely define our problem instance.

The initial J-schedule σ consists of a single block, in which jobs are included in the increasing order of their indexes. The earliest scheduled job 1 is the live emerging job which is followed by jobs 2–11 scheduled in this order. It is easy to see that the latter jobs form the kernel K in schedule σ. Indeed, all the 11 jobs belong to the same block, job 1 pushes the following jobs, and its delivery time is less than that of these pushed jobs. Hence, job 1 is the live emerging job in schedule σ. The overflow job is job 11, since it realizes the value of the maximum full completion time (the makespan) in schedule σ, which is $110 + 100 = 210$. Therefore, jobs 2–11 form the kernel in σ.

Note that the condition in Lemma 1 is not satisfied for schedule σ as its kernel K starts at time 100 which is more than $r(K) = 10$. Furthermore, the condition of Corollary 1 is also not satisfied for schedule σ, and it is not optimal. The optimal schedule S^* has the makespan 120, in which the live emerging job 1 is rescheduled behind all kernel jobs.

From here on, we use T^S for the makespan (maximum full job completion time) of J-schedule S and T^* (L^*_{max}, respectively) for the optimum makespan (lateness, respectively).

Lemma 2. $T^\sigma - T^* < p_l$ ($L^\sigma_{max} - L^*_{max} < p_l$), *where l is the live emerging job for kernel $K \in \sigma$.*

For our problem instance and the corresponding schedule σ, the above bound is almost reached. Indeed, $T^\sigma - T^* = 210 - 120 = 90$, whereas $p_l = 100$ ($l = 1$).

Note that Lemma 2 implicitly defines a lower bound of $T^\sigma - p_l$ derived from the solution of the non-preemptive J-heuristic, which can further be strengthen using the following concept. Let the delay for kernel $K \in \sigma$, $\delta(K,l)$ be $c_l - r(K)$ (l (o, respectively) stands again for the live emerging (overflow, respectively) job for kernel K). Then, the next lemma follows from the observation that $\delta(K,l)$ is another (more accurate than p_l) estimation for the delay of the earliest scheduled job of kernel K.

Lemma 3 *$L^* = T^\sigma - \delta(K,l)$ ($L_o(\sigma) - \delta(K,l)$, respectively) is a lower bound on the optimal job makespan T^* (lateness $L^*_{\max}$, respectively).*

Lemma 4 *J-heuristic gives a 2-approximate solution for $1|r_j,q_j|C_{\max}$, i.e., $T^\sigma/T^* < 2$.*

Proof. If there exists no live emerging job l for $K \in \sigma$, then σ is optimal by Corollary 1. Suppose job l exists; clearly, $p_l < T^*$ (as l has to be scheduled in S^* and there is at least one more (kernel) job in it). Then, by Lemma 2,

$$T^\sigma/T^* < (T^* + p_l)/T^* = 1 + p_l/T^* < 1 + 1 = 2. \tag{1}$$

□

4. Refining J-heuristic's worst-case estimation

From Lemma 2 of the previous section, we may see that the quality of the solution delivered by J-heuristic is somehow related with the maximum job processing time $p_{\max}$ in a given problem instance. If such a long job turns out to be the live emerging job, then the corresponding forced delay for the successively scheduled kernel jobs clearly affects the solution quality. We may express the magnitude $p_{\max}$ as a fraction the optimal objective value and derive a more accurate approximation ratio. It might be possible to deduce this kind of relationship priory with a good accuracy. Take, for instance, a large-scale production where the processing time of an individual job is small enough compared to an estimated total production time T.

If this kind of prediction is not possible, we can use the bound from Lemma 3 by a single application of J-heuristic and represent $p_{\max}$ as its fraction κ (instead of representing it as a fraction of an unknown optimal objective value). Then, we can give an explicit expression of the heuristic's approximation ratio in terms of that fraction. As we will see, J-heuristic will always deliver a solution within a factor of $1 + 1/\kappa$ of the optimum objective value. Alternatively, we may use a lower bound on the optimal objective value L^* from Lemma 3 (as T^* may not be known). Let $\kappa > 1$ be such that $p_l \le T^*/\kappa$, i.e., $\kappa \le T^*/p_l$. Since L^* is a lower bound on T^* ($L^* \le T^*$), we let $\kappa = L^*/p_l$, and thus we have that $\kappa \le T^*/p_l$, i.e., $\kappa = L^*/p_l$ is a valid assignment. Then, note that for any problem instance, κ can be obtained in time $O(n \log n)$.

Theorem 1 *$T^\sigma/T^* < 1 + 1/\kappa$, for any $\kappa \le T^*/p_l$.*

Proof. By Lemma 2,

$$T^\sigma/T^* < (T^* + p_l)/T^* = 1 + p_l/T^* \le 1 + 1/\kappa. \tag{2}$$

□

In the previous section's example, we had a very long live emerging job that has essentially contributed in the makespan of schedule σ. The resultant J-schedule gave an almost worst-possible performance ratio from Lemma 4 due to a significant intersection $\delta(K,l)$ (close to the magnitude p_l). We now illustrate an advantage of the estimation from Theorem 1. Consider a slightly modified instance in which the emerging job l remains moderately long (a more typical average scenario). A long emerging job 1 has processing time $p_1 = 10$, release time $r_1 = 0$, and the delivery time $q_1 = 0$. The processing time of the rest of the jobs is again 1. Latter jobs are released at time 5 and also have the same delivery times as in the first instance. The J-schedule σ has the makespan 120. The lower bound on the optimum makespan defined by Lemma 2 is hence $120 - 10 = 110$.

The approximation provided by J-heuristic for this problem instance can be obtained from Theorem 1. Based on Theorem 1, we use the lower bound 115 on T^* and obtain a valid $\kappa = T^*/p_l = 115/10 = 11.5$ and the resultant approximation ratio $1 + 1/11.5$. Observe that for our second (average) problem instance, J-heuristic gave an almost optimal solution.

5. An adaptive 3/2-approximation heuristic

In Section 2, we have mentioned two $O(n^2\log n)$ heuristic algorithms from references [19, 27] solving for our generic problem with the approximation ratios 3/2 and 4/3, respectively. In the previous section, we have described a more flexible approximation ratio that was obtained by a single application of J-heuristic.

In this section, we propose an $O(n\log n)$ heuristic that gives approximation ratio 3/2 for a large class of problem instances, which we will specify a bit later. This algorithm, unlike the above-mentioned algorithms, carries out a constant number of calls to J-heuristic (yielding thus the same time complexity as J-heuristic). Recall that the initial J-schedule σ is obtained by a call of J-heuristic for the originally given problem instance. By slightly modifying this instance, we may create alternative J-schedules with some desired property. With the intention to improve the initial J-schedule σ, and more generally, any J-schedule S, jobs in kernel $K = K(S)$ can be restarted earlier.

To this end, we *activate* an emerging job e for kernel K, *that is*, we force job e and all jobs scheduled after kernel K to be scheduled behind K (all these jobs are said to be in the state of activation for K). Technically, we achieve this by increasing the release times of all these jobs to a sufficiently large magnitude, say, $r(K) = \max_{j \in K}\{r_j\}$, so that when J-heuristic is newly applied, neither job e nor any job scheduled after K in S will surpass any job in K, and hence the earliest job in kernel K will start at time $r(K)$.

We call the resultant J-schedule a *complementary* to S schedule and denote it by S_l. Thus, to create schedule S_l, we just increase r_l to $r(K)$ and apply the heuristic again to the modified instance.

Our $O(n\log n)$ heuristic first creates schedule σ, determines kernel $K = K(\sigma)$, and verifies if there exists the live emerging job l; if there is no l, then σ is optimal (Corollary 1). Otherwise, it creates one or more complementary schedules. The first of these complementary schedules is σ_l. If job l remains to be an emerging job in schedule σ_l, then the second complementary schedule $(\sigma_l)_l$, obtained from the first one by activating job l for kernel $K(\sigma_l)$, is created. This operation is repeatedly applied as long as the newly arisen overflow job, that is, the overflow job in the latest created complementary schedule is released within the execution interval of job l in schedule σ (job l is activated for the kernel of that complementary schedule). The algorithm halts when either l is not an emerging job in the newly created complementary schedule or the overflow job in that schedule is released behind the execution interval of job l in schedule σ. Then, the heuristic determines the best objective value among the constructed J-schedules and halts.

Theorem 2 *The modified heuristic has the performance ratio less than* $3/2$.

Proof. In an optimal schedule S^*, either (1) job l remains to be scheduled before the overflow job o of schedule σ (and hence before all jobs of kernel $K = K(\sigma)$) or (2) l is scheduled after job o (and hence after kernel K).

Let E be the set of emerging jobs in schedule σ not including the live emerging job l. In case (1), either σ is already optimal or otherwise $E \neq \emptyset$, and some job(s) from set E are scheduled after kernel K in an optimal schedule S^* (so that job l and the jobs in K are rescheduled, respectively, earlier). Let $P = P(E)$ be the total processing time of jobs in E. Since job l stays before kernel K, $T^\sigma - T^* < P$ (this can be seen similarly as Lemma 2). Let (real) α be such that $P = \alpha p_l$. Since schedule S^* contains jobs of set E and job l, $T^* \geq \alpha p_l + p_l = (1+\alpha)p_l$. We have

$$T^\sigma/T^* < (T^* + \alpha p_l)/T^* = 1 + \alpha p_l/T^* \leq 1 + \alpha p_l/((1+\alpha)p_l) = 1 + \alpha/(1+\alpha). \quad (3)$$

Hence, if $\alpha \leq 1$ (i.e., $P \leq p_l$), then $T^\sigma/T^* < 3/2$.

Suppose now $P > p_l$. Then, $T^* > 2p_l$ and using again Lemma 2

$$T^\sigma/T^* < (T^* + p_l)/T^* < 1 + p_l/(2p_l) = 3/2. \quad (4)$$

It remains to be considered in case (2) when job l is scheduled after (all jobs from) kernel K in schedule S^*. We claim that schedule S^* is again "long enough," i.e., $T^* > 2p_l$. Indeed, consider the J-schedule σ_l. If σ_l is not optimal, then there exists an emerging job in S_l. Similarly as above, in schedule S^*, either (2.1) job l remains before $K(\sigma_l)$ or (2.2) l is scheduled after $K(\sigma_l)$.

In case (2.2), l must be an emerging job in σ_l. If the overflow job in kernel $K(\sigma_l)$ is released after time moment p_l, then $T^* > 2p_l$ as job l is scheduled after the jobs in $K(\sigma_l)$ in schedule $(\sigma_l)_l$. Otherwise, suppose the overflow job in schedule σ_l is released within time interval $(0,p_l)$ (note that it cannot be released at time 0 as otherwise would have originally been included ahead job l by J-heuristic). Without loss of generality and for the purpose of this proof, assume l is an emerging job in schedule σ_l, as otherwise the latter schedule already gives a desired approximation, similarly as in case (1). Because of the same reason, either schedule $(\sigma_l)_l$ gives a desired approximation or otherwise job l remains to be an emerging job (now, $(\sigma_l)_l$), and the heuristic creates the next complementary schedule $((\sigma_l)_l)_l$. We repeatedly apply the same reasoning to the following created complementary schedules as long as the overflow job in the latest created such schedule is released within time interval $(0,p_l)$. Once the latter condition is not satisfied, job l will be started at time moment, larger than p_l in the corresponding complementary schedule. Hence, its length will be at least $2p_l$. Moreover, an optimal schedule S^* must be at least as long as $2p_l$ unless one of the earlier created complementary schedules is optimal. Hence, one of the generated complementary schedules gives a desired approximation.

In case (2.1), if there is no emerging job in σ_l, then we are done. Otherwise, let E' be the set of emerging jobs in σ_l not including job l. Then similarly as for case (1), there are two sub-cases $P(E') \leq p_l$ and $P(E') > p_l$, in each of which a desired approximation is reached. The theorem is proved.

As to the time complexity of the modified heuristic, note that, in the worst-case, the overflow job in every created complementary schedule is released no later than at time p_l. Then, the algorithm may create up to $n-1$ complementary schedules, and its time complexity will be the same as that of the earlier-mentioned algorithms. However, it is clear that very unlikely, in an instance of $1|r_j,q_j|C_{\max}$, an "unlimited" amount of jobs are released before time p_l (that would be a highly restricted instance). In average, however, we normally would expect a constant number of such jobs, which, more restrictively, must be overflow jobs in the created complementary schedules (not belonging to kernel $K(\sigma)$). In this case, our heuristic will obviously run in time $O(n\log n)$. We have proved the following result:

Theorem 3. *The modified heuristic runs in time* $O(n\log n)$ *for any problem instance of* $1|r_j,q_j|C_{\max}$ *in which the total number of the arisen overflow jobs in all the created complementary schedules released before time* p_l *is no more than a constant* κ *(more brutally, for any instance in which the total number of jobs released before time* p_l *is bounded by* κ*).*

6. Conclusion

We have described efficient heuristic methods for the solution of a strongly *NP*-hard scheduling problem that, as we have discussed, has a number of important real-life applications. We have argued that it is beneficial as an analysis of the basic structural properties of the schedules created by J-heuristic for the construction of efficient heuristic methods with guaranteed worst-case performance ratios. As we have seen, not only J-heuristic constructs 2-optimal solutions in a low-degree polynomial time, but it is also flexible enough to be served as a basis for other more efficient heuristics. The useful properties of J-schedules were employed in our flexible worst-case performance bound of Section 4 and in the proposed, in Section 5, heuristic algorithm with an improved performance ratio. The latter heuristic is adaptive in the sense that it takes an advantage of the structure of an average problem instance and runs faster for such instances.

We believe that J-schedules possess further useful yet undiscovered properties that may lead to the disclosure of yet unknown insights of the structure of the related problems with release and delivery times. This kind of study was reported in recently published proceedings [8, 9] for the case of a single processor and two allowable job release and delivery times. It still remains open whether basic properties described in these works can be generalized for a constant number of job release and delivery times and for the multiprocessor case. At the same time, some other yet not studied properties even for a single processor and two allowable job release and delivery times may exist. The importance of such a study is emphasized by the fact that the basic single-machine scheduling problem is strongly *NP*-hard and that the version with only two allowable job release and delivery times remains *NP* hard [8].

Author details

Nodari Vakhania

Address all correspondence to: nodari@uaem.mx

Center of Research and Science, UAEMor, Mexico

References

[1] Adams J, Balas E, Zawack D. The shifting bottleneck procedure for job shop scheduling. Management Science. 1988;**34**:391–401

[2] Bratley P, Florian M, Robillard P. On sequencing with earliest start times and due-dates with application to computing bounds for $(n/m/G/F_{max})$ problem. Naval Research Logistics Quarterly. 1973;**20**:57–67

[3] Brinkkotter W, Brucker P. Solving open benchmark instances for the job-shop problem by parallel head–tail adjustments. Journal of Scheduling. 2001;**4**:53–64

[4] Carballo L, Vakhania N, Werner F. Reducing efficiently the search tree for multiprocessor job-shop scheduling problems. International Journal of Production Research 2013;**51**(23–24):7105–7119. DOI: 10.1080/00207543.2013.837226

[5] Carlier J. The one-machine sequencing problem. European Journal of Operations Research. 1982;**11**:42–47

[6] Carlier J, Pinson E. An algorithm for solving job shop problem. Management Science. 1989;**35**:164–176

[7] Carlier J, Pinson E. Jackson's pseudo preemptive schedule for the $Pm/r_i,q_i/C_{max}$ problem. Annals of Operations Research 1998;**83**:41–58

[8] Chinos E, Vakhania N. Polynomially solvable and NP-hard special cases for scheduling with heads and tails. In: Recent Advances in Mathematics and Computational Science. (MCSS 16). Barcelona, Spain 2016. pp. 141–145. Available from: http://www.wseas.us/e-library/conferences/2016/barcelona/MCSS/MCSS-17.pdf

[9] Chinos E, Vakhania N. Scheduling jobs with two release times and tails on a single machine. International Journal of Mathematical Models and Methods in Applied Sciences 2016;**10**:303–3089. Available from: http://www.naun.org/main/NAUN/ijmmas/2016/a782001-aan.pdf

[10] Condotta A, Knust S, Shakhlevich NV. Parallel batch scheduling of equal-length jobs with release and due dates. Journal of Scheduling. 2010;**13**:463–477

[11] Del Ser, Javier (Ed.). A harmony search approach for the selective pick-up and delivery problem with delayed drop-off. In Harmony Search Algorithm. Berlin Heidelberg: Springer; 2016. pp. 121–131

[12] Della Croce F, T'kindt V. Improving the preemptive bound for the single machine dynamic maximum lateness problem. Operations Research Letters. 2010;**38**:589591

[13] Garey MR, Johnson DS. Computers and intractability: A guide to the theory of NP-completeness. San Francisco: Freeman; 1979

[14] Garey MR, Johnson DS, Simons BB, Tarjan RE. Scheduling unit–time tasks with arbitrary release times and deadlines. SIAM Journal on Computing. 1981;**10**:256–269

[15] Gharbi A, Labidi M. Jackson's semi-preemptive scheduling on a single machine. Computers & Operations Research. 2010;**37**:2082–2088

[16] Glover F. Tabu-search: A tutorial. Interfaces. 1990;**20**:74–94

[17] Grabowski J, Nowicki E, Zdrzalka S. A block approach for single-machine scheduling with release dates and due dates. European Journal of Operational Research. 1986;**26:**278–285

[18] Graham RL, Lawler EL, Lenstra JL, Rinnooy Kan AHG. Optimization and approximation in deterministic sequencing and scheduling: A survey. Annals of Discrete Mathematics. 1976;**5**:287–326

[19] Hall LA, Shmoys DB. Jacksons rule for single-machine scheduling: Making a good heuristic better. Mathematics of Operations Research 1992;**17**:22–35

[20] Ivens P, Lambrecht M. Extending the shifting bottleneck procedure to real-life applications. European Journal on Operations Research. 1996;**90**:252–268

[21] Jackson JR. Scheduling a production line to minimize the maximum tardiness. Los Angeles, CA: Management Science Research Project, University of California; 1955

[22] Kirkpatrick S, Gelant CD, Vecchi MP. Optimization by simulated annealing. Science. 1983;**220**:924–928

[23] Lawton G. Genetic algorithms for schedule optimization. AI Expert. 1992;23–27

[24] McMahon G, Florian M. On scheduling with ready times and due dates to minimize maximum lateness. Operations Research. 1975;**23**:475–482

[25] Ow PS, Morton TE. Filtered beam search in scheduling. International Journal of Production Research. 1988;**26**:35–62

[26] Perregaard M, Clausen J. Parallel branch-and-bound methods for the job-shop scheduling problem. Annals of Operations Research. 1998;**83**:137–160

[27] Potts CN. Analysis of a heuristic for one machine sequencing with release dates and delivery times. Operations Research. 1980;**28:**1436–1441

[28] Toth P, Vigo D, editors. Vehicle Routing Problem (SIAM Monographs On Discrete Mathematics and Applications, vol. 386). Philidelphia, PA: SIAM; 2002

[29] Schutten JMJ. Practical job shop scheduling. Annals of Operations Research. 1998;**83**: 161–177

[30] Schrage L. Obtaining optimal solutions to resource constrained network scheduling problems, unpublished manuscript (March 1971)

[31] Simons B. Multiprocessor scheduling of unit-time jobs with arbitrary release times and deadlines. SIAM Journal of Computing. 1983;**12**:294–299

[32] Simons B, Warmuth M. A fast algorithm for multiprocessor scheduling of unit-length jobs. SIAM Journal of Computing. 1989;**18**:690–710

[33] Vakhania N. A better algorithm for sequencing with release and delivery times on identical processors. Journal of Algorithms. 2003;**48**:273–293

[34] Vakhania N. Single-machine scheduling with release times and tails. Annals of Operations Research. 2004;**129**:253–271

[35] Vakhania N. Scheduling jobs with release times preemptively on a single machine to minimize the number of late jobs. Operations Research Letters. 2009;**37**:405–410

[36] Vakhania N. Branch less, cut more and minimize the number of late equal-length jobson identical machines. Theoretical Computer Science. 2012;**465**:49–60

[37] Vakhania N. A study of single-machine scheduling problem to maximize throughput. Journal of Scheduling. 2013;**16**(4):395–403

[38] Vakhania N, Shchepin E. Concurrent operations can be parallelized in scheduling multiprocessor job shop. Journal of Scheduling. 2002;**5**:227–245

[39] Vakhania N, Werner F. Minimizing maximum lateness of jobs with naturally bounded job data on a single machine in polynomial time. Theoretical Computer Science. 2013;**501**:7281

[40] Vakhania N, Perez D, Carballo L. Theoretical expectation versus practical performance of Jackson's Heuristic. Mathematical Problems in Engineering. 2015;**2015**: ID 484671. DOI: http://dx.doi.org/10.1155/2015/484671

[41] Vakhania N, Hernandez JA, Alonso-Pecina F, Zavala C. A Simple heuristic for basic vehicle routing problem. Journal of Computer Science Technology Updates. 2016;**3**(2):38–44. DOI: http://dx.doi.org/10.15379/2410-2938.2016.03.02.04

Section 3

Heuristic Techniques and Applications

Chapter 5

Advanced Particle Filter Methods

Roi Yozevitch and Boaz Ben-Moshe

Additional information is available at the end of the chapter

http://dx.doi.org/10.5772/intechopen.69236

Abstract

This chapter presents a set of algorithmic methods based on particle filter heuristics. We start with an introduction to particle filters, which covers the main motivation and related works. Then, the generic framework for particle filter algorithm is presented, followed by two important use cases regarding indoor positioning and multitarget tracking; for both problems, modified particle filter algorithms are presented followed by experimental results, implementation remarks, and a discussion. Finally, a short list of conclusion and future work are presented.

Keywords: particle filter, localization, navigation heuristics, position accuracy estimation, GNSS jamming, indoor navigation, multitarget tracking

1. Introduction

Among the heuristic techniques and filters available to the researcher, the "particle filter" technique is one of the most flexible to use. Unlike the Kalman filter on its variations (especially the Extended and Unscented Kalman filters, namely EKF and UKF), the particle filter is neither restricted to Gaussian a posterior distribution nor to a unimodal solution. The number of problems that can be described by a particle filter are numerous. Why is particle filter considered a heuristic technique? The answer is obvious: In essence, the particle filter is a nonparametric way to sample the desired probabilistic space. Real-world probabilistic spaces are often complex and cannot rely upon Gaussian/convex assumptions. Sampling such an arbitrary space utilizing finite numbers of particles is naturally an approximation. Hence, the particle filter should be considered as a generic heuristic technique for modeling complex probabilistic spaces.

1.1. Motivation

In the last decade, a massive amount of research has been devoted to both autonomous cars and unmanned aerial vehicles (UAVs). Part of this research includes multiagent localization (e.g., swarms of robots). The contemporary autonomous car is equipped with a wide range of sensors which requires an intelligent data fusion to construct a reliable reality map. One must remember that autonomous cars are a mission critical system; that is, the system must work all of the time. Such system cannot solely rely on global positioning system (GPS), since it is occasionally not available (e.g., dense urban canons and city tunnels). Furthermore, in those systems, estimating the error bounds is not just a convenient feature. In December 2011, an American UAV landed in a hostile enemy environment, over 200 km from its original route. This drone was equipped with the state-of-the-art military navigation system. This example (later known as Iran-U.S. RQ-170 incident [1]) demonstrates the crucial importance for modeling the error space based on data from several sensors.

While fully autonomous cars are still a far vision, current new cars are required to have active-safety systems in order to get a full safety rating (five-star safety level). Those systems are capable to detect the car position in the lane and warn the driver about pedestrians and other cars.

Particle filters can address all of the above challenges. In this chapter, we present new algorithmic improvements to estimate the system's error bounds, to localize and track multiagents and more. Rapid advances in hardware acceleration and the intense use of parallel computing (e.g., graphics processing unit, GPU) across the board are perfect for implementing the particle filter in many scenarios.

In this chapter, we focus on two abstract problems that the state-of-the-art particle filters are dealing with. The first problem is how to reduce the number of particles without losing (a lot) of knowledge. The second problem is how to both localize and track more than one agent simultaneously. Those abstract algorithmic challenges are demonstrated via two case studies.

1.2. Related works

The concept of simulating particles started in the 1960s [2] to address nonlinear parabolic partial differential equations arising in fluid mechanics. The term "particle filter" was first defined in the mid 1990s [3]; however, other researchers have used the terminology of "sequential Monte Carlo" [4]. In the last two decades, a considerable amount of research work was devoted to develop various heuristics based on particle filters [5–8]. Positioning algorithms are often based on particle filters as it is a robust method for performing sensor fusion [9, 10]. In order to improve the expected runtime performance, several researchers have developed a GPU-based parallel-methodology for particle filters [11–13]. It is important to note that a particle filter is a generic technique and is being used to solve (approximate) a wide range of nonlinear problems including video stabilization, tracking, and multitarget tracking (MTT) [14, 15]. Finally, particle filters are becoming a common high-level heuristic which is being used in many autonomous robotic applications [16–18] allowing both robustness and improved error-bound estimations.

http://dx.doi.org/10.5772/intechopen.69236

2. Particle filter: general heuristic

As stated above, the particle filter is a member of the nonparametric multimodal Bayesian filters family. In the particle filter case, the posterior is estimated by a finite number of parameters (particles). These particles are represented as $\chi_t := x_t^{[1]}, x_t^{[2]}, \ldots, x_t^{[N]}$, where N is the number of particles. A belief function, $bel(x_t)$, is evaluated for each particle. This function serves as the particle's weight (importance). Thus, $\{x_t^{(K)}, (w_t^{(K)},) : K \in \{1, \ldots, N\}\}$. The importance weight is proportional to the likelihood of a specific particle [19]:

$$x_t^{[K]} \sim p(x_t | z_{1:t}, u_{1:t}) \times w_t^{(K)} \tag{1}$$

In Eq. (1), $z_{1:t}$ and $u_{1:t}$ are the sense and action functions, respectively. The action function u_t moves the particles at time t. The movement is usually derived from odometry (wheel encoding, pedometers). A fundamental characteristic of the action function is the accuracy reduction of each particle. Since any real-world movement contains (to a certain degree) noise, moving a particle **decreases** certainty regarding its state. The sense function, z_t, does exactly the opposite. This function evaluates the particle's likelihood based on its sensors (vision, Inertial Measure Unit - IMU, etc.). Assuming the particle measures distance from n known landmarks, one can evaluate the weight of each particle p as:

$$z(x_t) \sim \sum_{1}^{n} f(x | \mu, \sigma^2) \tag{2}$$

where f represents the Gaussian function:

$$f(x | \mu, \sigma^2) = \frac{1}{\sigma\sqrt{2\pi}} e^{-(x-\mu)^2/2\sigma^2} \tag{3}$$

The value x represents the measured distance to the nth landmark and μ represents the theoretical distance between the known landmark and the particle position. The closer a particle to its true position, the value $abs(x - \mu)$ diminishes and the particle's weight increases. Thus, the sensor function **increases** certainty regarding its state. This process is also called Monte Carlo localization (MCL) [19].

The particle filter is a Bayesian, multimodal, nonparametric estimation tool. In order to fully understand this concept, several terms must be clarified:

- The Bayesian property implies that the estimation at t_1 is derived from the estimation at t_0.
- The multimodal feature implies that unlike Kalman filters, there can be more than a single plausible solution.
- The nonparametric property implies the posterior is not restricted to a Gaussian (or other parametric) probability density function (PDF).

Data: Sensor data, Map (optional)
Result: Improved position
1. Init: Distribute a set P of M particles in the *ROI*;
2. Estimate the velocity vector $\vec{v}_t$ from the sensor measurements (e.g., gyroscope, encoder, pedometer...);
3. **for each** *particle* $p \in P$ **do**
    4. Approximate the **action function** $u_t(p)$ from $\vec{v}_t$;
    5. Update p-position according to $u_t(p)$;
    6. Evaluate the belief (weight) function: $w(p)$ based on the known landmarks and map restrictions (Map Matching);
7. Resample P according to the likelihood (weight) of each particle;
8. Compute best position in $P \in ROI$ as $pos(P)$;
9. **Report** $pos(P)$;
10. Approximate the error estimation $err(P)$;
11. if (err(P) < *ROI*) go to 2 else go to 1;

Algorithm 1: Simple Particle Filter Algorithm.

Properties 2 and 3 mean that the PDF is constructed by the particles themselves, therefore, any arbitrary function can be described that way—there is not a single best estimate. A particle can be in position A or B with equal likelihood. Thus, a particle filter is well suited for scenarios where one needs to estimate its location within a building with two (or more) identical rooms.

Each particle is a state vector (similar to the Kalman Filter) with a dimension n. Most localization problems define each particle to a set of a position and a velocity vectors:

$$x_t^{[K]} = \left\{position, \overrightarrow{velocity}\right\} \tag{4}$$

A 2D problem demands for $n = 4$ and a 3D problem demands for $n = 6$. One can also include the particle's orientation (crucial in vehicle localization) and other features as well.

2.1. The generic particle filter algorithm

The algorithm presented is a generic PF localization algorithm. One seeks to find an accurate absolute position from noisy measurements. The action function is usually derived from the odometer (e.g., wheel's encoder).

2.2. Reporting the best solution

As opposed to the traditional Kalman filter where the current state vector is also the filter's best guess, a particle filter holds N different solutions (some more plausible than others). How can one determine the "best" particle? The following are the most common approaches:

- The "best" particle will be computed as the center-of-mass of all particles. This is achieved by averaging all the particles.
- A more sophisticated approach is to compute a weighted average of all particles. Each particle reports its likelihood (weight), so this is relatively straight forward to implement. One should carefully notice that in both methods, the "best" estimate is almost never a

valid particle, only an average of valid particles. When external restrictions exist on the particle themselves, the produced "best estimate" may not obey those restrictions.

- One can simply pick the particle with the highest weight. This is the easiest approach to adopt.
- The first approach can be fused to a single method; choose the particle with the highest weight and compute a weighted center of mass solution around it.

The above methods have one thing in common—they all assume a single solution exists and they seek to find it. In other words, they do not take advantage of the inherent multimodal characteristic of the filter itself. Assuming there are two equally likely solutions, the first two methods will produce a bad guess and the last two will produce only one good solution. Such scenarios do exist when tracking more than one agent and we will discuss those types of scenarios in the following sections.

2.3. Particle filter flaws

While relatively easy to understand and implement, the naive particle filter method suffers from several flaws. As explained above, the naive algorithm is incapable of handling multiagent scenarios. It is true that most localization algorithms seek a single best estimate but this is not true of all of them.

The second point concerns the algorithm runtime complexity. Each particle can be computed independently of the other, thus $O(|N|)$, where $n = |N|$, is the number of particles. Doubling N will double the expected runtime. Alas, the configuration space grows exponentially with respect to the state vector's size. As such, extending a 2D PF to 3D is very complicated.

Finally, as always, real-world scenarios are very different from the sterile PF examples found in the literature. A PF sense function is usually explained utilizing distance from several **known** landmarks where each distance has a Gaussian noise with $\mu = 0$. This scenario does simplify the math but does not describe real-world sensors.

The following section is dedicated to real-world indoor localization problem.

3. Smartphone-based indoor navigation

Contemporary navigation heavily relies on Global Navigation Satellite Systems (GNSS) such as the American GPS and the Russian GLONSS. GNSS signals, however, cannot be used inside buildings. Therefore, indoor navigation depends on other type of sensory data.

3.1. Problem state

Given a smartphone receiver in a well-defined region of interest (ROI), find its most plausible location using only the phone's inherent sensors (IMU, camera, etc.).

The best candidate for this task is the smartphone WiFi module. Each WiFi router (transmitter) sends a signal (also called a WiFi-beacon) at ≈ 10 Hz. Since the WiFi-received signal strength indication (RSSI) decreases with the distance between the router and the phone, one can utilize this information as the conventional landmark. The WiFi scenario differs from the classic (known) landmark sensors in three main aspects:

1. The routers' position is not known. Moreover, in a conventional shopping mall there could be over 100 different WiFi routers. New routers are continuously added and old routers are discarded.

2. The RSSI is not solely affected from the distance. The phone orientation (how the antenna is held), obstruction (walls and the human body), and the building geometry are more important. This means that far signals can be received with a relatively high RSSI while near signals can be received with relatively low RSSI.

3. Although WiFi signals travel at ≈ c (speed of light), the receiver occasionally detects them with a 1–2 second delay. This is due to the way a WiFi scan is performed over the available channels (commonly 13 in 2.4 GHz). At pedestrian speed, 2 s of delay may not be an issue. However, when the user crosses a critical section, this can lead to significant errors.

The above flaws make the sense function hard to intelligently construct. Not only is the RSSI a poor distance indicator, the landmarks (WiFi routers) may be obsolete.

3.2. RF finger printing

In the last two decades, there has been massive research on indoor position, see Refs. [20, 21] for general surveys on indoor positioning technologies. In most cases, some sort of RF finger printing algorithm was implemented [22]. Indoor location services are offered on mobile platforms as Google-Android, Apple-IOS, and Windows-Mobile, and they are commonly based on 3G/4G cellular networks, combined with WLAN fingerprinting (WiFi, Bluetooth (BLE)). The expected accuracy of such systems is commonly 5–30 m at 0.3–1 Hz. In the scope of this chapter, we assume that some kind of location service is available for the user and we present a set of particle filters designed to improve the accuracy and robustness of such services.

3.3. Map constraints

Most navigation applications use an underlying map on which the user position is presented. Such maps can be used by the particle filter algorithms for improving the evaluation of each moving particle with respect to the map constraints (i.e., walls). **Figure 3** presents an example of a floor plan with about 10% walls—yet, using such a map combined with the user movement (action function) allows the particles to converge rapidly. For simplicity, the map constraints are presented here in a binary mode which basically divides the region of interest to areas in which the user can be (white) and restriction zones (black) in which the user may not be. Naturally, one can think of a finer model with several levels or even continuance values. Yet, in most cases the binary model is sufficient and allows for a simple implementation.

3.4. Intelligent weight evaluation

Occasionally, momentary misclassifications will happen due to obstructions (e.g., walls). Hence, one must also consider the particle's history and incorporate it into the weight function. The strengths of this approach are twofold: First, a positive feedback will cause more probable particles to become better in time. Second, this method reduces to minimum the influence of those momentary errors. We set $0<k<1$ to be the ratio between the current estimation and the history weight. A more robust solution will be achieved with lower *k*. Noisy environments should favor the history. Note that *k* is the equivalent to the Kalman *K* gain. Each estimation problem has a different optimal *k* values:

$$weight(x_t^{[K]}) = k \times sense(x_t^{[K]}) + (1 - k) \times weight(x_{t-1}^{[K]}) \tag{5}$$

where $weight(t)$ is the average of the current sense function with all of its history.

Why is it important? Why not increase the number of particles?

Given the number of particles $M \to \infty$, there is a mathematical proof of the convergence of the filter [19]. However, "infinite" number of particles is neither practical nor efficient. Moreover, as stated above, the number of particles grows exponentially with the problem's dimension; one should seek for the minimum optimal number of particles and the rigorous methods for determining that number which are rare. We have used 100, 500, 1000 and 2500 particles throughout the experiments. **Figure 1** demonstrates how the more the particles being used, the smaller the average (steady) error is. We denote "average error" as the average weighed distance between all the particles and the true position. Moreover, as elaborated in Section 3.4, since each particle have no memory of its history, a momentary misclassification can cause significant error as depicted in **Figure 1**. One hundred particles are usually considered as a practical lower bound. Below this number, the solution will often diverge. On the other hand, 5000 particles (and above) produce errors very similar to 2500 particles. In essence, there is a trade-off between the number of particles and the algorithm's accuracy. Although the trade-off is not linear (increasing the number of particles from 100 to 200 will yield much higher improvement than increasing the number of particles from 1000 to 1200), the accuracy is a monotonically increasing function of the number of particles.

One can have both a small number of particles (efficiency) and a very accurate algorithm by implementing the intelligent weight function (Eq. (5)). When the particle's history is taken into account, the errors caused by the small amount of particles are overcome. **Figure 2** proves this thesis. Given a small number of particles (100), the suggested method improves the solution considerably. However, as expected, the improvement is barely noticed for much bigger *N* values.

What do these graphs mean? As we see, these graphs tell a very interesting story. At first glance, one might suspect this method is not "kosher" since the likelihood of an arbitrary particle was already expressed in the resampling phase—the higher the weight (likelihood) a particle has, the higher the chance for it to be resampled over again. Therefore, incorporating its last weight value seems wrong—creating a deformed unrealistic probability space. However, as clearly demonstrated in **Figure 2**, utilizing this method, especially for a small number

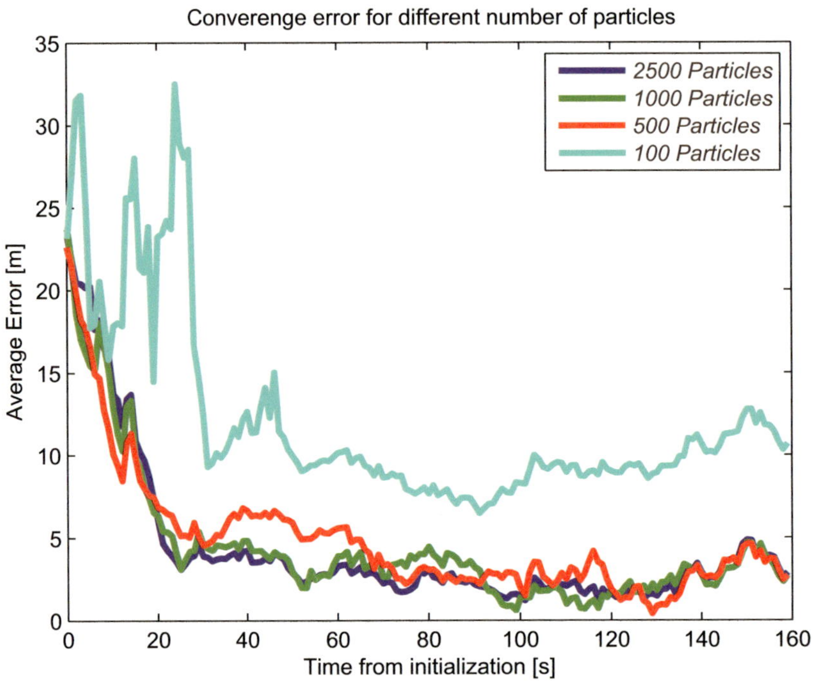

Figure 1. Average error for different numbers of particles. The more the particles being used, the smaller the average error.

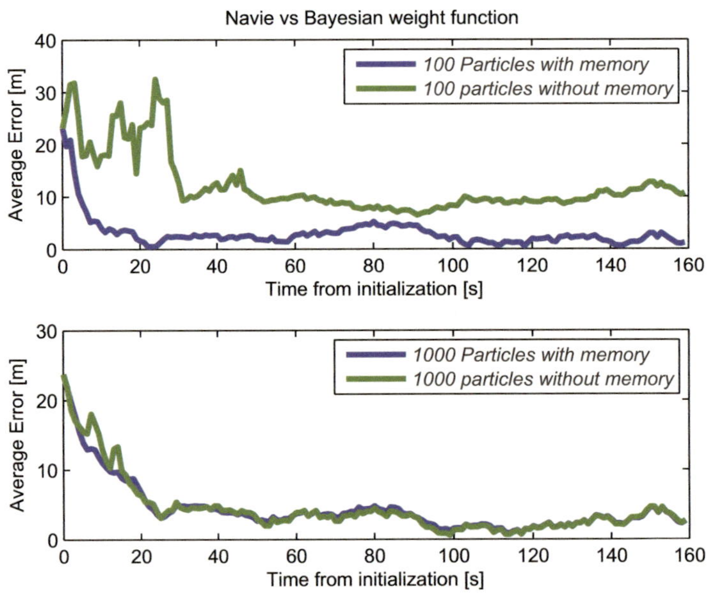

Figure 2. Naive versus Bayesian weight function. For small number of particles (100), the use of each particle history improves the solution and reduces the average error. For 1000 particles, the difference is unnoticed.

of particles (≈100 particles), significantly improves the results. This improvement, however, is barely noticed when the number of particles is higher (1000 particles).

While particle filter algorithms are nonparametric [19], they still demand for quite configurations and their efficiency heavily lies in an intelligent "sense" function. Evaluating such functions is not an easy task and one should be closely familiar with the domain to do so. A better, more accurate, "sense" function will yield more accurate results.

3.5. Simulation results of smartphone positioning

In this section, we present a set of simulations representing the presented particle filter in the setting of smartphone indoor navigation using floor-map constraints, RF positioning, and a pedometer. In **Figures 3–5**, we consider a "standard building" with a size of 10×20 m with about 10 rooms, the overall restriction area (i.e., walls) is about 10% of that area. The path is shown as a polygonal line, the real position is marked as a solid dark dot located on the path and the approximated position is marked as a lighter dot. The simulation uses the following

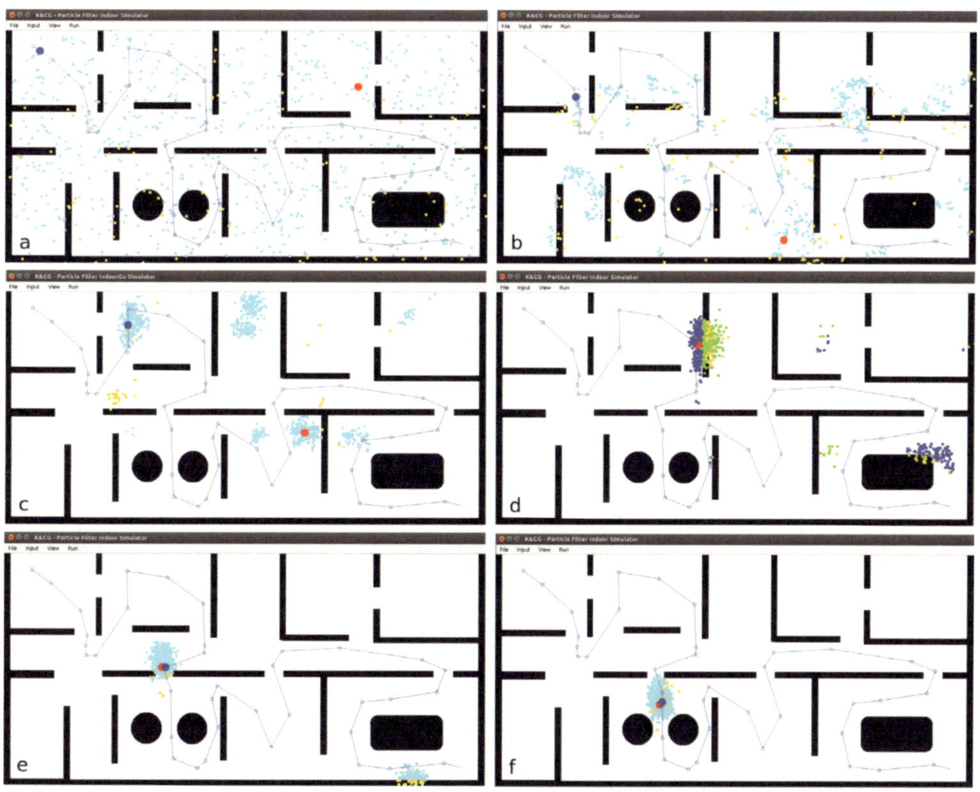

Figure 3. Particle filter in action: 800 particles were randomly located in the building (a) with no RF positioning service. Using pedometer combined with compass and a building floor map, the particles rapidly form few small clusters (b and c). (d and e) The correct solution (cluster) is computed yet the expected error is still relatively large—as there is a second (wrong) cluster of particles. (f) The algorithm converges and the expected accuracy is high.

Figure 4. Particle filter in action: 100 particles were randomly located in the building (a), a WiFi positioning service was used for fast converges (b and c). All the particles converged to the correct position (d).

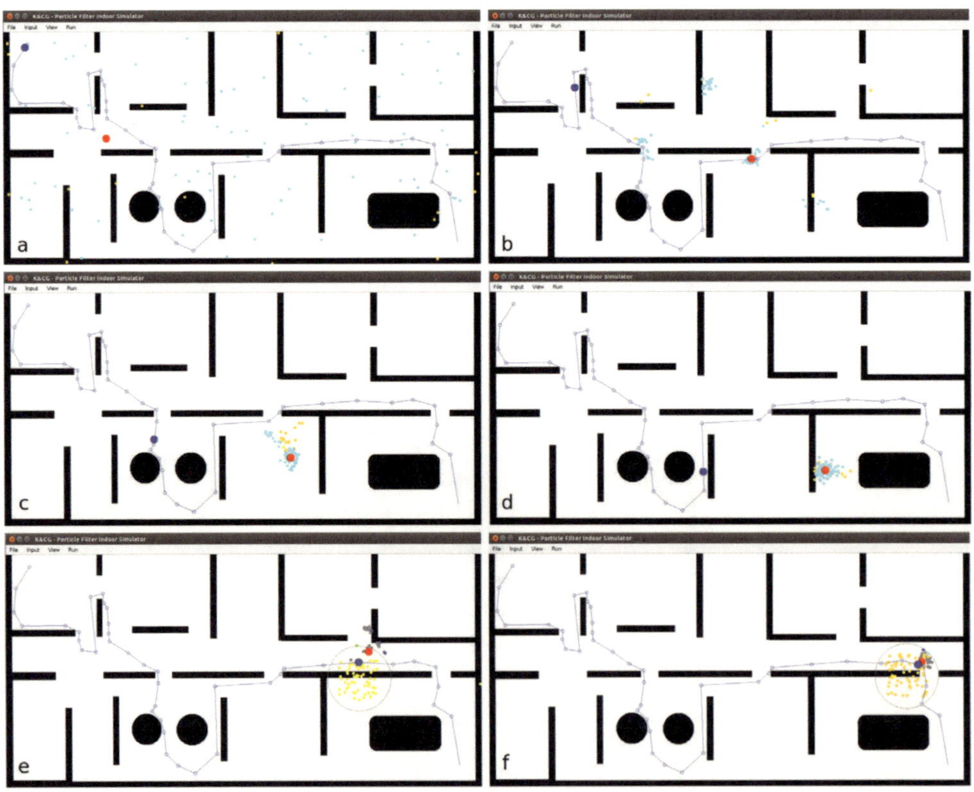

Figure 5. Particle filter in action: 100 particles were randomly located in the building (a). No RF positioning service is leading to a wrong converges (b–d), due to undersampling—the number of particles is too low. Using RF positioning (e and f), the correct position was found.

parameters: theWiFi expected position error is 5 m, the pedometer expected error is 20% in length, and 10 in angle.

In order to demonstrate the particle filter algorithm in the setting of indoor positioning, we first present the case (**Figure 3**) in which there is no RF (i.e., WiFi) positioning service. This case can also be seen in situations where the accuracy of the positioning service is larger than the region of interest. We then present (**Figures 4** and **5**) the more general case in which RF positioning service is available. Using this service, the particle filter converges rapidly even with significantly smaller set of particles.

3.6. 3D particle filter algorithm

Prior to this point, we have mainly considered the 2D case of the mobile phone indoor position algorithm. In this section, we will generalize the particle filter algorithm to a 3D case of multifloor buildings. In general, a building navigation is often referred to as 2.5D—in which the floor is assumed to be of a discrete value. Two modifications are needed in order to generalize the algorithm for 3D:

1. The floor(s) map should have an additional color (probability) representing the probability of floor change in each location: e.g., near by the elevator or the stairs, this probability (color) will be relatively high.
2. The action function should have an elevation (Δz) approximation. This functionality is commonly computed via a barometric pressure sensor. One should remember that these sensor are extremely sensitive to height differentiation (i.e., one cannot deduce the correct floor based on their value but one can confidently deduce floor change by inspecting the sensor's data derivative).

3.7. Overcoming the kidnapped robot problem

Since particle filters are not restricted to a single peak PDF, they can handle an ambiguous location scenario: e.g., two (almost) identical rooms in a hall. The filter maintains two clusters of particles in the candidate locations. Convergence is assumed when the receiver exits one of the rooms. Alas, a robust convergence to the true location is not guaranteed in a noisy environment, in particular, with a wrong map or biased sensors. Many indoor navigation algorithms suffer from this very problem (see **Figures 3** and **4** for such examples). City mall maps are occasionally changed and WiFi routers are moved from their previous location. These phenomena can throw a filter to converge to a wrong location (e.g., different floor). This is a major problem since standard particle filters hardly recover from a wrong position after they converge, in particular, since floor change is always accompanied with a major shift in the barometer sensor. Even if the receiver "wants" to converge to the true location, it cannot do so unless it is nearby an elevator or escalator. It is important to mention that this is a real problem in the realm of Inertial Navigation System (INS) and many algorithms will occasionally reset their value and start over. If one wishes to avoid such system resets, this issue must be addressed properly.

Wrong location convergence is very similar to another known problem, the kidnapped robot problem [19]. In the latter, we assume all the particles correctly converged to the true robot's position. However, a foe (intentional or not) kidnapped the robot and placed it outside the convergence area. If no particle exists in the robot's new location, a true convergence is not possible. Therefore, a small portion of the particles (≈10% or less) is allocated in each phase to evenly respread in the ROI. Thus, the algorithm has a viable probability to reconverge to the true location. In our example, we evenly spread the particles in different floors.

4. Multiagents localization and tracking

Multitarget tracking (MTT) is a well-known problem in the field of image processing and estimation [23]. In particular, addressing the MTT problem utilizing particle filter techniques has been done previously [24, 25]. The scope of the problems MTT addresses is usually visual tracking. In this section, however, we would like to present a very easy-to-implement particle filter-based algorithm to tackle a nonvisual multiobject localization problem.

Section 2.2 presents several ways to report the estimated location based on the particles' distribution. As explained, all the methods assumed a single true solution, i.e., a single-agent localization. When two (or more) clusters of particles present, the algorithm either chooses the "best" solution from one of the clusters or attempts to average them all to produce a false answer somewhere in between them. When two (or more) clusters represent true position of several agents, we seek an algorithm which can both localize and track all of those agents.

4.1. Problem of interest

Our problem of interest consists of several radiant sources and several sensors which can detect this radiation. The aim is to localize, track, and estimate the numbers of radiant sources in the region. The radiation can be noise (sound waves), fire (heat or smoke), light, electromagnetic fields, etc. We chose to describe an interesting electromagnetic source—GNSS jammers.

4.1.1. GNSS jammers localization and tracking

The importance of GNSS is unquestionable. We rely on it more and more for both civilian and military uses. Attacking this system can cause a great deal of harm to any modern society. GNSS jammers jam the carrier frequency of the GNSS receiver (hence their name) by adding (transmitting) white noise to it. This process degrades the receiver signal-to-noise ratio (SNR) to a point where the receiver is unable to report its position, a phenomenon usually referred to as "losing fix." A 10 W jammer can paralyze GNSS receivers over a radius of a few hundred meters. Jamming interference can be detected by a degradation of the received satellites' SNR values. **Figure 6** demonstrates a typical jamming interference.

As **Figure 6** demonstrates, there exists a positive correlation between the receiver's SNR and its distance from the jammer. The black vertical line represents the jamming range; beyond that distance, the receiver is not affected by the jamming interference.

The reason why the jammer's location is interesting is twofold:

- First, the "losing fix" phenomena are similar to the uncertainty principle: when the receiver is far away from the jammer, it is not affected by it and produces a reliable GNSS location. When the receiver is very close to the jammer, it cannot report its location since it has no fix.

- While it is easy to model a GNSS jammer as an omnidirectional antenna which degrades the received signals evenly in all directions, in reality, most jammers emit only in a certain direction.

As explained above, the problem of interest consists of both the radiant sources and the sensors. In our context, the emitting sources are the GNSS jammers, whereas the sensors are the GNSS receivers (e.g., smartphones) which can detect and report the satellites' received SNR. A strong SNR indicates no jamming interference. As the detected SNR decreases, the distance between the sensor and the jammer also decreases. This observation leads to the conclusion that if one can sample the SNR in the entire ROI, one can create a "heat map" of the most interfered points. Those points will serve as good candidates as the jammers' location. However, sampling the entire ROI is not viable in many cases, mainly due to map constraints. One needs to deduce the heat map form only a partial sampling.

4.1.2. Heat map

A plausible approach to tackle the emitting sources' problem is to define for each sensory record (sensor in time) a simplified probabilistic map (of the ROI) which represents the likelihood for the jammer to be at any point of the ROI. All the likelihood maps are combined one on top of the other to develop the heat map. **Figure 7** demonstrates such a heat map.

The experiment scenario is depicted in the left side of **Figure 7**. The red star represents the jammer's position. The yellow line represents the sensor's track. At each point, the sensor's SNR was recorded. As the sensor moves away from the jammer, its SNR increases and vice versa. Each such point creates a likelihood map. One can see that maximum intensity occurs in the vicinity of the real jammer.

When no jammer is presented, the maximum heat region will be outside the ROI, as expected. **Figure 8** demonstrates this phenomenon.

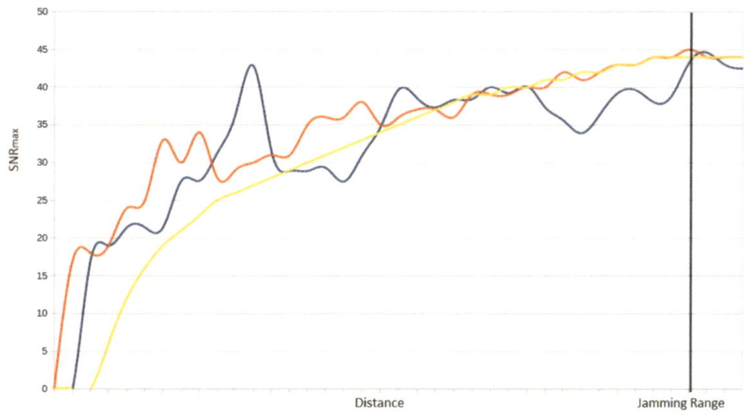

Figure 6. GNSS jamming SNR degradation. As the receiver approaches the jammer, its SNR decreases. As the receiver becomes farther away, its SNR increases. The yellow line represents the theoretical behavior, whereas the other colors represent real-world recoding figures.

This algorithm suffers from several inherent flaws:

- It assumes an omnidirectional pattern of the jammer. In other words, the algorithm cannot cope with more complex transmitting patterns.
- Since the algorithm has no notion of time, it is almost impossible to detect a nonstationary jammer.
- Much more important, the algorithm assumes the jammer's transmitting power is given. This, of course, is never the case in the real world.
- When two (or more) jammers are presented, the algorithm will not be able to differ between them (unless they are widely separated).

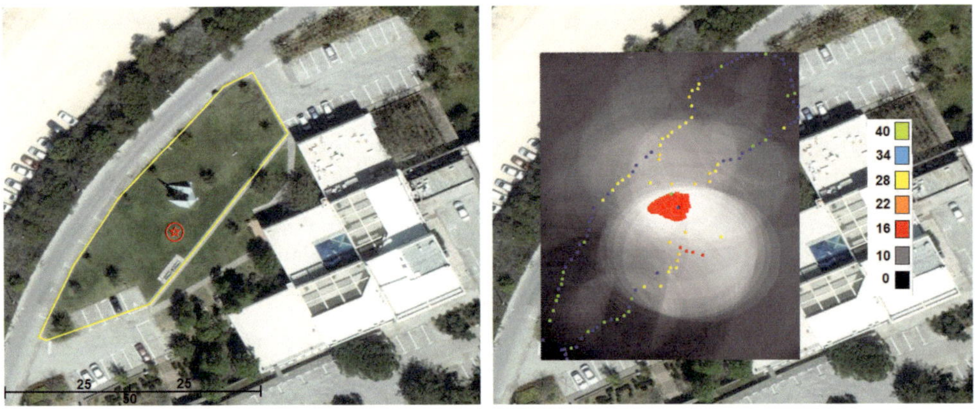

Figure 7. A heat map algorithm: Left: A field experiment in which a single jammer was located at the red star and the yellow polygon presents the sensor (GNSS receiver) path. Right: The samples of the sensor are presented in colored dots —the scale presents the maximal signal of the QNSS satellites. The heat map is presented in gray scale colors—the brightest region in the ROI is marked in red and overlaps the actual location of the jammer. In case of a single (fixed) jammer, this solution might be sufficient.

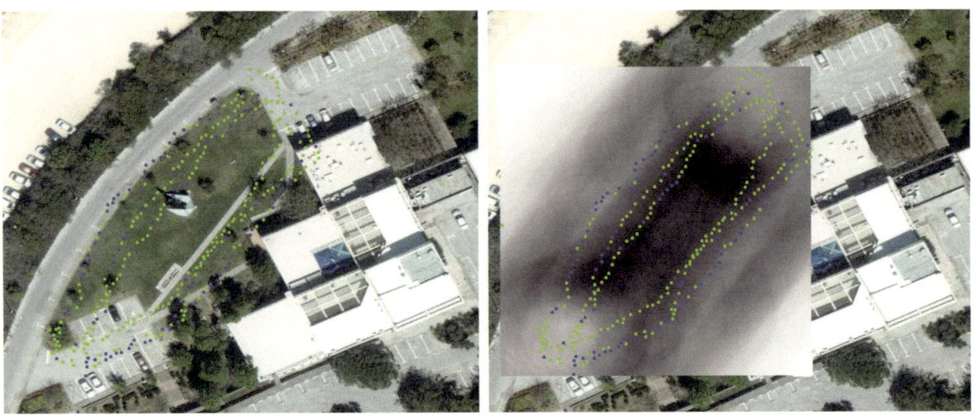

Figure 8. A heat map algorithm: No active jammer. Left: All samples. Right: The brightest regions of heat map are at the upper left and lower right corners. Since no jammer exists, the algorithm assumes it is outside the ROI.

http://dx.doi.org/10.5772/intechopen.69236

Data: *ROI*, sensor data
Result: *GNSS* jammer location
1. Init: Distribute a set P of n particles in the *ROI*;
2. **while** *P is not converged* **do**
    3. **for each** *particle* $p \in P$ **do**
        4. Approximate the **action function** $u_t(p)$ from $\vec{v}_t$;
        5. Update p-position according to $u_t(p)$;
        6. Evaluate the belief (weight) function: $w(p)$ based on the sensors input.
    7. Resample P according the likelihood (weight) of each particle;
8. Compute best position in $P \in ROI$ as $pos(P)$;
9. **Report** $pos(P)$;

Algorithm 2: Single *GNSS* jammer tracking.

In order to tackle all of the above flaws, a more probabilistic approach should be taken. A (modified) particle filter can efficiently address the multiagent localization and tracking problem with a relatively small number of particles.

4.2. Single agent tracking algorithm

The following sections describe a robust method to detect, localize, and track several emitters in the ROI. For the sake of clarity, we first assume a single jammer scenario. Several jammers tracking algorithm will be explained in the next section. The proposed algorithm does not assume a known number of emitters or their exact transmitting power. Moreover, this algorithm copes well with scenarios where the jammers are mobile and may overlay each other. Since we seek to know the position (and velocity) of the jammer(s), each particle is defined as a possible jammer with a specific velocity, position, and transmitting power. The weight of each particle will be proportional to the number of sensors (smartphones) consistent with it. This approach assumes almost no prior knowledge regarding the jammers in the ROI. Since each particle holds a velocity vector, the algorithm can also track moving jammers. The formal description of the algorithm is given below:

As explained above, each particle represents a jammer. The initialization happens in line 1: each particle is a jammer with a different transmitting pattern. Its weight is proportional to the jammer's probability of being in a specific location. One can compute this probability as the sum of Gaussian distributions (since the pattern is known).

Convergence occurs when the longest distance between every two particles does not exceed a certain threshold. If no jammer exists in the ROI, the particles will not converge and the algorithm will not report a position. This algorithm tracks well a single jammer. However, the inherent nature of the particle filter prevents it from operating well in several jammers scenario. **Figure 9** demonstrates this problem. In this figure, one can see two jammers, each with a different strength and pattern, as represented by the black lines. The little squares represent several dozen sensors (smartphones). Although two jammers transmit in this scenario, all the particles converged to a single jammer.

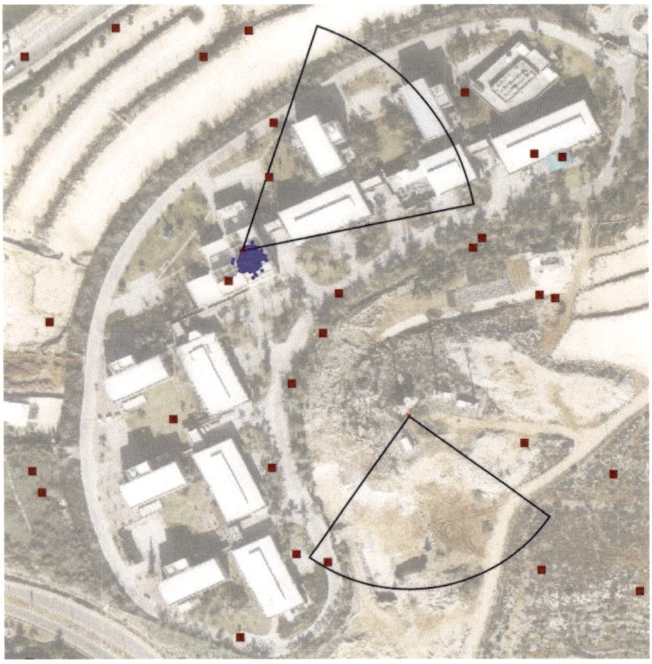

Figure 9. A single jammer localization. Although two jammers are active simultaneously, the particles converged only to one of them.

4.2.1. Unimodal versus multimodal

Although particles filters are not restricted to unimodal single peak PDFs, the resampling process itself tends to converges to a **single** value. Thus, two different clusters of particles (representing two jammers) will eventually converge to only one of the jammers due to the inherent resampling process. Should this was a typical clustering problem, a K-mean algorithm [26] would work well because the resampling process tends to favor one cluster over the others. This cluster will be the last one to survive and the other clusters (jammer) will be ignored. A typical particle filter algorithm can hold multimodal two-peak PDF, only as an intermediate phase. Multiagent tracking calls for a slightly different approach.

Data: ROI, sensor data
Result: *GNSS* jammers' locations
1. Init: Define *Jammers* to be an empty set of Jammers;
2. **while** *JammerDetection(ROI)* **do**
    3. Let J_i be *findjammer(ROI)*;
    4. Add J_i to the *Jammers;*
    5. Update the ROI to be $ROI - ROI(J_i)$
6. return *Jammers;*

Algorithm 3: A generic algorithm for Multi Agent Localization.

4.3. Multiagent tracking algorithm

The multiagent tracking algorithm is very similar to Algorithm 2. The main difference is a more sophisticated approach toward convergence. After the algorithm converged to a single jammer, the algorithm respread particles outside the region of interference. The first set of particles is "assigned" to the first jammer and will track after it. The second set of particles will converge to another jammer relatively quickly. This happens due to the fact that the second set of particles is not affected by the first jammer. The formal description of this algorithm is given below.

Line 2: We denote *JammerDetection*(*ROI*). It is a Boolean function which returns true if the probability of having a jammer in the ROI exceeds a certain threshold.

Lines 3 and 4: Algorithm 2 was utilized to find the most probable jammer in the ROI. As mentioned above, Algorithm 2 reports a jammer position only after all the particles converged. If a jammer is detected, it will be added to the list (line 4).

Line 5: If a jammer was detected (line 3), the algorithm respreads particles outside the region of interference of the detected jammer. Calculating this region is easy since each particle holds the antenna pattern and the jamming transmitting power.

The next figures validate the algorithm's correctness. **Figure 10** depicts a two-jammer tracking scenario, each jammer having a different antenna pattern.

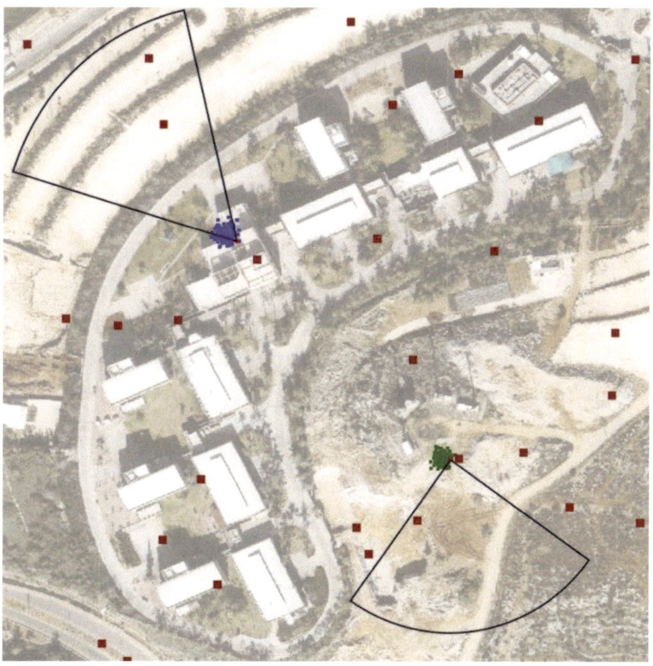

Figure 10. A single-jammer localization. Two jammers are active simultaneously and the algorithm converged to both of them.

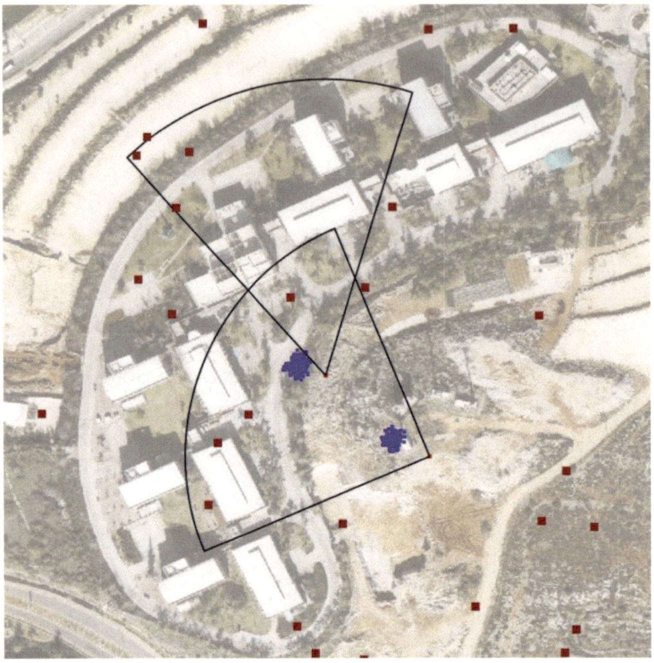

Figure 11. A single-jammer localization. Although two jammers are active simultaneously, the particles converged only to one of them.

Figure 11 shows an overlapping scenario. The interference regions of the jammers partly overlap and yet, the algorithm tracks each jammer separately.

4.4. Implementation remarks

The proposed framework for multiagent localization and tracking produces relatively accurate results, even with a small number of particles and sensors. While increasing the number of particles depends solely on computing power, increasing the number of sensors can be much more challenging and occasionally impossible. The results described here were achieved with 500 particles (for each jammer) and less than 30 sensors (smartphones).

5. Future research

Recent advances in technology such as autonomous driving, the Internet of Things (IoT), and bioinspired robotics require sophisticated and robust methods for computing probabilistic functions. In many cases, the problems of interest are NP-hard problems or have a real-time (or online) requirements and therefore cannot be solved accurately and efficiently using deterministic algorithms. Moreover, many mission critical systems are required to approximate not just the "state" (e.g., position and velocity) but suggest a tight bound for the expected error of the reported solution (i.e., an accuracy level). Such error-bound approximation is important for autonomous platforms in which performing well in 99% of the time is insufficient. Heuristics based on particle filters allows a robust sensor fusion while maintaining the implementation relatively simple. Using such methods one can report the expected accuracy level (error). Using the modifications suggested in this work, one can significantly improve the expected runtime of a particle filter algorithm which makes it suitable even for real-time vision-based localization problems. For future work, we suggest that the need for robustness and real-time accurate results will require the use of massive parallel computation platforms such as GPU. Such platforms can allow an independent and parallel computing core for almost each particle and, therefore, to allow speedups of 10–100 times over existing solutions. Other research challenges include: designing particle filters on a sensor level—just as implementation of Kalman filter is common in embedded sensors. Finally, there is an important problem of setting and fine-tuning the parameters of a generic particle filter to a specific problem in the most suitable way. This research challenge can be seen as a double-stage particle filter: higher level particle filter seeks to improve its parameters while the lower level solves the problem of interest using a particle filter which uses the above parameters. Such a self-tuning heuristic might allow for a massive use of particle filter algorithms just as deep learning has allowed a greater and more efficient use of neural networks.

Author details

Roi Yozevitch* and Boaz Ben-Moshe

*Address all correspondence to: yozevitch@gmail.com

Ariel University, Ariel, Israel

References

[1] Hartmann K, Steup C. The vulnerability of UAVs to cyber-attacks—An approach to the risk assessment. In: 2013 5th International Conference on Cyber Conflict (CyCon). IEEE; 2013. pp. 1–23

[2] McKean HP. A class of Markov processes associated with nonlinear parabolic equations. Proceedings of the National Academy of Sciences. 1966;**56**(6):1907–1911

[3] Del Moral P. Non-linear filtering: Interacting particle resolution. Markov Processes and Related Fields. 1996;**2**(4):555–581

[4] Liu JS, Chen R. Sequential Monte Carlo methods for dynamic systems. Journal of the American Statistical Association. 1998;**93**(443):1032–1044

[5] Crisan D, Rozovskii B. The Oxford Handbook of Nonlinear Filtering. Oxford University Press, Oxford, England; 2011

[6] Flury T, Shephard N. Bayesian inference based only on simulated likelihood: Particle filter analysis of dynamic economic models. Econometric Theory. 2011;**27**(05):933–956

[7] Doucet A, De Freitas N, Gordon N. An introduction to sequential Monte Carlo methods. In: Sequential Monte Carlo Methods in Practice. Springer, Berlin, Germany; 2001. pp. 3–14

[8] Van Der Merwe R, Doucet A, De Freitas N, Wan E. The unscented particle filter. In: NIPS. Vol. 2000. Denver, CO, USA. 2000. pp. 584–590

[9] Gustafsson F. Particle filter theory and practice with positioning applications. IEEE Aerospace and Electronic Systems Magazine. 2010;**25**(7):53–82

[10] Nurminen H, Ristimaki A, Ali-Loytty S, Piché R. Particle filter and smoother for indoor localization. In: 2013 International Conference on Indoor Positioning and Indoor Navigation (IPIN). IEEE; 2013. pp. 1–10

[11] Montemayor AS, Pantrigo JJ, Sánchez Á, Fernández F. Particle filter on GPUS for real-time tracking. In: ACM SIGGRAPH 2004 Posters. ACM; 2004. p. 94

[12] Hendeby G, Hol JD, Karlsson R, Gustafsson F. A graphics processing unit implementation of the particle filter. In: 2007 15th European Signal Processing Conference. IEEE; 2007. pp. 1639–1643

[13] Chao M-A, Chu C-Y, Chao C-H, Wu A-Y. Efficient parallelized particle filter design on cuda. In: 2010 IEEE Workshop on Signal Processing Systems (SIPS). IEEE; 2010. pp. 299–304

[14] Farahmand S, Roumeliotis SI, Giannakis GB. Set-membership constrained particle filter: Distributed adaptation for sensor networks. IEEE Transactions on Signal Processing. 2011;**59** (9):4122–4138

[15] Rui Y, Chen Y. Better proposal distributions: Object tracking using unscented particle filter. In: Proceedings of the 2001 IEEE Computer Society Conference on Computer Vision and Pattern Recognition, 2001. CVPR 2001., Vol. 2. IEEE; 2001. pp. 768–793

[16] Montemerlo M, Thrun S, Koller D, Wegbreit Ben, et al. Fastslam: A factored solution to the simultaneous localization and mapping problem. In AAAI/IAAI; 2002. pp. 593–598

[17] Petrovskaya A, Thrun S. Model based vehicle detection and tracking for autonomous urban driving. Autonomous Robots. 2009;**26**(2-3):123–139

[18] Niknejad HT, Takeuchi A, Mita S, McAllester D. On-road multivehicle tracking using deformable object model and particle filter with improved likelihood estimation. IEEE Transactions on Intelligent Transportation Systems. 2012;**13**(2):748–758

[19] Thrun S, Burgard W, Fox D. Probabilistic Robotics. MIT Press, Cambridge, Massachusetts (United States); 2005

[20] Gu Y, Lo A, Niemegeers I. A survey of indoor positioning systems for wireless personal networks. IEEE Communications Surveys & Tutorials. 2009;**11**(1):13–32

[21] Zekavat R, Buehrer RM. Handbook of Position Location: Theory, Practice and Advances. Vol. 27. John Wiley & Sons, Hoboken, New Jersey; 2011

[22] Honkavirta V, Perala T, Ali-Loytty S, Piché R. A comparative survey of WLAN location fingerprinting methods. In: 6th Workshop on Positioning, Navigation and Communication, 2009. WPNC 2009. IEEE; 2009. pp. 243–251

[23] Bar-Shalom Y. Multitarget-multisensor Tracking: Advanced Applications. Norwood, MA: Artech House; 1990. p. 391

[24] Hue C, Le Cadre J-P, Pérez P. Tracking multiple objects with particle filtering. IEEE Transactions on Aerospace and Electronic Systems. 2002;**38**(3):791–812

[25] Okuma K, Taleghani A, De Freitas N, Little JJ, Lowe DG. A boosted particle filter: Multitarget detection and tracking. In: European Conference on Computer Vision. Springer; 2004. pp. 28–39

[26] Hartigan JA, Wong MA. Algorithm as 136: A k-means clustering algorithm. Journal of the Royal Statistical Society. Series C (Applied Statistics). 1979;**28**(1):100–108

Chapter 6

On the Use of Hybrid Heuristics for Providing Service to Select the Return Channel in an Interactive Digital TV Environment

Marcos César da Rocha Seruffo,
Ádamo Lima de Santana,
Carlos Renato Lisboa Francês and
Nandamudi Lankalapalli Vijaykumar

Additional information is available at the end of the chapter

http://dx.doi.org/10.5772/intechopen.69615

Abstract

The technologies used to link the end-user to a telecommunication infrastructure, has been changing over time due to the consolidation of new access technologies. Moreover, the emergence of new tools for information dissemination, such as interactive digital TV, makes the selection of access technology, factor of fundamental importance. One of the greatest advantages of using digital TV as means to disseminate information is the installation of applications. In this chapter, a load characterization of a typical application embedded in a digital TV is performed to determine its behavior. However, it is important to note that applications send information through an access technology. Therefore, this chapter, based on the study on load characterization, developed a methodology combining Bayesian networks and technique for order preference by similarity to ideal solution (TOPSIS) analytical approach to provide support to service providers to opt for a technology (power line communication, PLC, wireless, wired, etc.) for the return channel.

Keywords: heuristics, model decision making, service provider, return channel, interactive digital TV

1. Introduction

The interactive digital TV (DTV) environment allows a new class of services around television content that was to broadcast, where interactive programs can be employed allowing user interaction. The interaction implies totally different approaches to reflect and produce television content. In addition, one must keep in mind that such issue makes telecommunication infrastructures to deal with new load of data.

In this aspect, service providers have to plan the implantation of technology, based on these new demands that will be a part of computing environments. The diversity of broadcast applications and the usage of an interactive channel, as external communication in the Brazilian context, lead to a case-study with the objective to consider the social inclusion specified in Brazilian Presidential Decree No. 4901.

It is even more necessary as the Brazilian digital TV system (SBTVD) presents as a promising alternative when considering digital inclusion, since the television, besides being present in more than 90% of Brazilian homes, according to national survey by household sample of Brazilian Institute of Geography and Statistics (IBGE) [1]. It is also available to virtually all social classes, in all regions of Brazil, which is not true in the case of other communication devices, such as computers.

Therefore, one can consider that the digital TV has a great scope and it should not be restricted to a mere process of improving the quality of transmission. One must also consider it to be used as a tool for digital inclusion, naturally with strong possibility of interactivity.

In this context, a universe of activities involving production of audio/visual content to include applications that allow the user to interact with the interactive TV applications has been growing. The possibility to offer applications to viewers by means of interactive digital television (iTV) [2] originates a new production chain involving programs and applications development of interactive character. Based on this aspect, service providers should be concerned with the diversity of applications and services that can be offered.

One of the main challenges, for social and digital inclusion through digital TV, is to enable the population, mainly located in areas of difficult access and low-income, to gain access to services such as t-health and t-education. Besides, it becomes a major challenge to access providers to use the traditional TV broadcast, the interaction with multiscreens (tablets, PC, TV, smartphones, etc.) allowing access with different digital services, to enable facilities such as purchases via online, chats with or without video, etc. However, this challenge implies on making networks available with a larger capillarity, in particular, when comparing to services available now.

Thus, it is fundamental to address the issue of first mile, i.e., the first technology with which a user connects to a telecommunication network; this term is used synonymously with technology access that ensures the interactivity (return channel) service. Studies must be conducted to service providers to have an idea of system performance characteristics. In order to secure this, scenarios must be studied and understood so that applications embedded in SBTVD can be used by end-users. Besides, solutions must be devised in order to facilitate providers to predict possible problems in the system.

Research should be conducted considering the following features: return channel and quality of service (QoS). Besides, such features must be taken into account in a combined manner with applications, amount of interactions that such applications require, as well as other aspects for ensuring effectiveness to deal with significant volume of services providing interactivity.

As a contribution, a provision of service strategies for selecting return channel within interactive digital TV environment is proposed in this chapter. This approach is based on a combination of measurements and analytical/artificial intelligence models, enabling decision making from a set of QoS parameters. With respect to measures, test results are obtained for measuring the delay, throughput, jitter, active connections, response time, data dropped, and number of retransmissions from access technologies. With respect to the analytical/computational intelligence models, two decision-making approaches—Bayesian network (BN) and technique for order preference by similarity to ideal solution (TOPSIS)—have been deployed to determine the best choice from the alternatives studied.

The selection of TOPSIS and Bayesian networks is encouraged by several factors, such as ease of implementation, use in several solutions (as shown in Section 2), experience of the research group in the use of these models, results obtained from the combination of these models, and the use of a hybrid proposal ratifies the excellence of the proposed model. It is necessary to reinforce that the proposal discussed here is quite generic and flexible making is easier to consider another parameters or technologies and thus adapting it to be prepared for the other kinds of decision making.

2. Related work

Based on constant advancement in technologies, several studies published in the areas of heuristics, service provider, digital TV, access technologies, and methods for decision making show that strategies for providing service to select the return channel are in the spotlight.

Usually, digital TV systems make use of the layered architecture to be represented. Lower layers provide services to upper layers. Architectures are similar but different with respect to modulation, coding, compression, transmission, running applications, and adopted middleware. In particular, for Brazil, the adopted middleware is known as Ginga.

According to Ref. [3], iTV systems allow a new variety of services over broadcast TV content. Therefore, user interaction through digital TV apps is possible. This implies in a new means to manipulate the content (from the user's point of view), because of this, stimulate a different form to produce and think about TV. This chapter presents interactive service provider architecture for iTV systems, from a service-oriented architecture and guaranteeing a standardized communication among client apps and services with interactivity.

SBTVD and its characteristics are discussed in Ref. [4]. It elaborates the analysis of several aspects with respect to the definition of SBTVD and relates the electronics industry's impact on its productive chain. It also identifies features and functions that are to be considered to be implemented in the system and even goes further by discussing the potential of sales of digital signal receivers.

Another paper [5] gave a relevant contribution by showing a variety of studies that addressed the connection between the end-user and telecommunication infrastructure. Authors in Ref. [6] address the concern in the behavior of networks given the increase in the number of end-users with access to systems like asymmetric digital subscriber line (ADSL), cable modem, wireless, power line communication (PLC), and optical fiber.

Reviewed literature showed technologies employed as a return channel for interactive digital TV. For example, based on the number of active subscribers, several models were designed and simulated to evaluate the performance of the system's capacity [7]. It brought evidences that WiMAX would perfectly fit as a return channel for digital TV interactive application. In Ref. [8], the tests use PLC as a return channel to test how effective it is for applications such as e-health and e-learning.

Traditional TV sets have been enhanced with new services due after digital TV has been introduced [9]. For example, set-top boxes enable access to Internet to send emails. This new approach allows interaction of the viewers with TV stations. The most important contribution of Ref. [9] is the analysis whether an ad-hoc wireless network is feasible to be used as a return channel as such networks are cheap and flexible.

Among the range of access technologies available in the market, the selection of access technology to be used by the service provider is the subject much discussed in the literature. As in Ref. [10], that uses the stochastic control technique, Markov decision process (MDP) studies and examines the relationship between optimal decisions that should be applied by the service provider.

Literature also shows that infrastructure for telecommunication must consider its improvement, as it is clear that there is an increase in the number of digital TVs if bottlenecks are to be avoided. Some methods have been suggested in Refs. [11, 12] to control such bottlenecks due to heavy telecommunication traffic. The method suggested is to enable access for volatile traffic and this is based on sample monitoring.

There are several tools to monitor and control and these may be employed to measure the system load and evaluate how bottlenecks can be avoided. In this sense, it becomes necessary to understand multicriteria decision-making methods.

Authors in Ref. [13] present an overview of various approaches to multicriteria decision making by comparing their performances, which can be used as a basis for the study of models employed for decision making.

One approach for the first mile problem to select user's connection can be found in Ref. [14]. It is based on multicriteria analysis and can be considered as a combination model as it addresses issues such as multicriteria ranking, knapsack-like problems, hierarchical clustering, and morphological synthesis.

Heuristics for multicriteria decision making have been widely used, as shown in Ref. [15], with several papers addressing algorithms for selecting the return channel in heterogeneous environments, such as Refs. [16–21], with different kinds of models.

Bayesian networks are graphical models for reasoning based on uncertainty, where nodes represent the variables (discrete or continuous) and arcs represent the direct connection between them. From the set of computational intelligence models surveyed in the literature, Bayesian Networks were chosen to model decision making to extract knowledge of a typical iTV application.

http://dx.doi.org/10.5772/intechopen.69615

The use of Bayesian networks with multicriteria decision-making methods is found in the literature, like Ref. [22], in which the authors show a problem of multicriteria decision making. The authors aim is to select the most suitable solution (given many alternatives). The idea is to propose a method that centers on the person since the "weight" given to each criterion is defined according to the features of the person. The solution is based on Bayesian network (BN) and analytic hierarchy process (AHP) method, the chart of the BN and the probabilities associated with nodes are designed to convert the knowledge of the specialists on the choice of an alternative.

In Ref. [23], the author presents a decision model to determine weights for the application, using a multi-attribute decision-making model based on Bayesian networks. Critical technique, dasiaBayesian networkspsila, is used to determine values for the weights, which combined prior information (other expertspsila knowledge, or numerical simulation, etc.) with expertspsila knowledge.

According to Ref. [24], "the weight in technique for order preference by similarity ideal solution (TOPSIS) is given by experts or decision makers. The value of weight would be influenced by expertspsila subjective judgments. A slight difference in value of weights may result in diversity of order of alternatives. In this chapter, a Bayesian method for the decision of weight for Multi-attribute decision-making model with interval data is introduced. The value of weight is decided by a priori information (other expertspsila knowledge, or numerical simulation, etc.) and experts' knowledge (or decision makerspsila experience/preference)." This paper is an example of the hybrid solution, using TOPSIS and BN in MADM.

To develop this chapter, a thorough literature survey on TOPSIS either standalone or hybridized with other heuristics/machine learning models was done. Papers like Refs. [25–30] show different types of use of TOPSIS as heuristic for decision making in the most diverse areas. Though, it is currently a hot research topic in the academic community; however, some gaps need attention which include the lack of studies using a heuristic, based on multicriteria analysis, using data collected, testing implementations on real devices, implementation of these heuristic in open platforms, mounting a consolidated database from simulation scenarios, using the TOPSIS method from a weight vector based on simulation tests, not experts, and comparison of different technologies that are already consolidated in the market.

Thus, the proposal discussed in this chapter contemplates the highlighted gaps by presenting a strategy for providing service to select the access technology for iTV environment. Therefore, the service provider can analyze the best technology to be used in a real scenario. For this, models are used for decision making based on Bayesian networks and TOPSIS.

3. Models for multicriteria decision making

When there are conflicting aims that may omit optimal solutions, decision making comes into picture as it can lead to a good solution. Multicriteria methods become important as they support decision making. According to Ref. [31], decision making can be simply described as an effort to solve the dilemma of conflicting goals. In problems concerning decision making, a decision maker usually assists in the process by listing several important criteria and analytical methods may be employed to aid in such decisions. There are two analytical approaches: American and European.

The North American approach is mainly represented by analytic hierarchy process (AHP) developed by Thomas Lorie Saaty. The European approach has a wider range of multicriteria decision methods, such as TOPSIS, elimination and choice translating reality (ELECTRE), measuring attractiveness by a categorical-based evaluation technique (MACBETH), among others [24].

From an extensive bibliographical survey in the area of decision making, TOPSIS was chosen due to its easy implementation, good behavior in mathematical tests performed, and solutions to be widespread in several areas, as in Refs. [24, 32–34].

Thus, studies were conducted with a view to decision making based on two components: (a) computational intelligence based on Bayesian networks; (b) multicriteria analysis based on TOPSIS.

4. Tests

Once the models that would be used were selected, a typical scenario was set for transmission of digital content, and a server was configured to respond to the user requests, simulating an iTV service infrastructure. Thus, characterization of the load of a typical digital TV was obtained. **Figure 1** shows the assembled infrastructure, with a transmission layer, responsible for transmitting the television programs for broadcast and interactive applications.

The application is received and executed in the user layer, which has a TV with a set-top box connected and access technology for a return channel. The infrastructure of the return channel is represented in the layer service provider and can be wired and wireless, leaving it to the provider to decide which technology is to be employed.

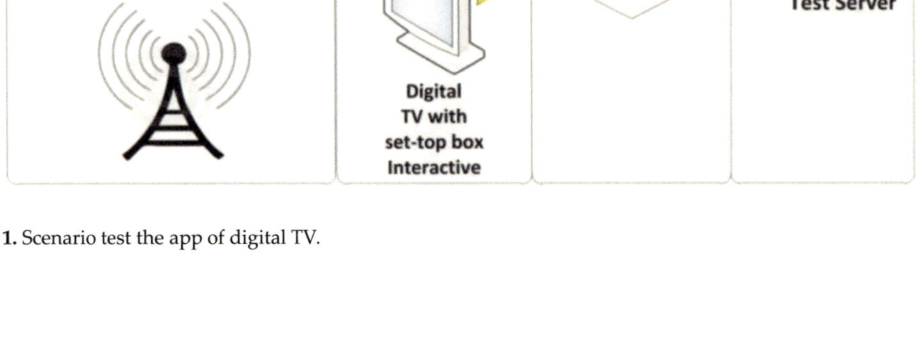

Figure 1. Scenario test the app of digital TV.

The layer of the test server is responsible for responding to requests from tests, with only the application server, which has the function of helping in the measurement criteria used for decision making.

The assembly of the aforementioned scenario was based on extracting measures of a typical network of digital TV. The application used in these tests was developed by the research group of this article, and is called DTV-Educ 2.0 [35].

The purpose of this application, a chat conversation, is to make it available for regular television program, so that a student who is watching television can make classroom questions in real time or even conduct group work with other students.

Figure 2 shows a screenshot of the developed application running on OpenGinga (Ginga emulator platform) during a conversation. It presents the history of messages exchanged between participants in the chat during a television program.

4.1. Characterization of load application

To characterize the load application in the network, tests were performed where two real users, for 10 min, exchanged messages via the chat provided by the application.

All application information was recorded during the conversation via a spy program network, and **Table 1** summarizes the measured statistical results of this application.

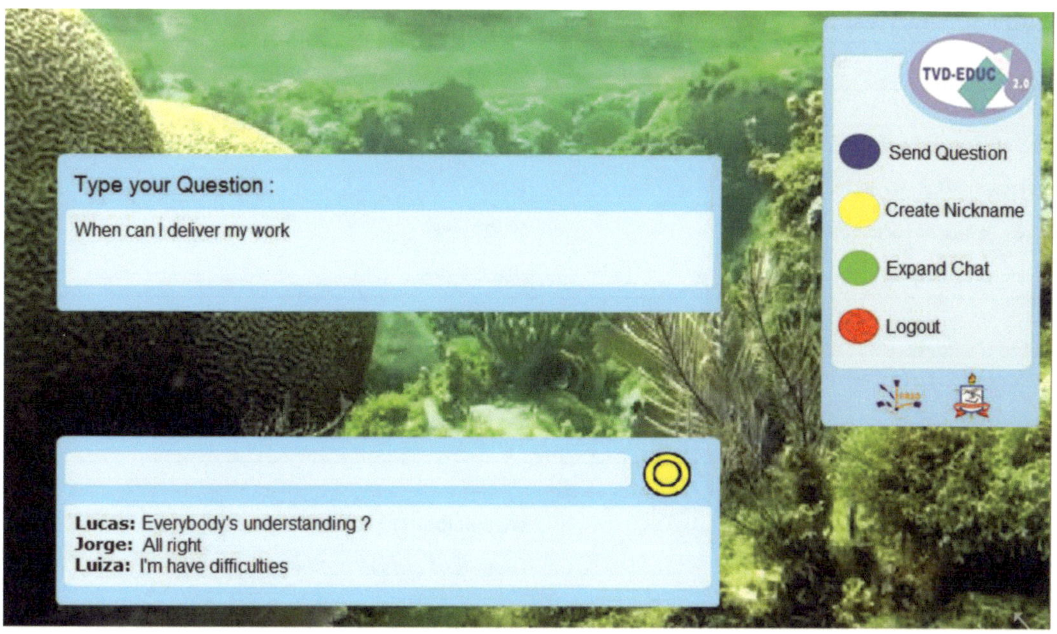

Figure 2. Application DTV-Educ 2.0 during a chat.

The measured data in **Table 1** were used for configuring the application in a simulation scenario. It is noteworthy that this application when compared with other types of traditional applications does not occupy the network much, because its traffic is only in plain text that is typed by users. In general, the applications used in digital TV environment present this behavior.

From the characterization of the DTV load application, other parameters that would be inserted in the simulation environment were set.

4.2. Definition of applications and parameters

After characterization of load application, it was necessary to conduct a research on flow commonly used on the Internet. The idea is to make the environment of a user utilizing an interactive application in as real scenario as possible.

Therefore, three streams that were used in simulation tests were defined: (i) application of video (video conferencing), (ii) application of voice over IP (VoIP), and (iii) typical application of digital TV (DTV-Educ 2.0). These three applications aimed to model traffic used by typical customers who use the Internet, and the first two were taken from Ref. [36].

The probability of some configuration parameters within digital TV application was obtained (from empirical studies) to characterize the traffic load and was fed as input to the simulator. The specification of the traffic load for the application DTV-Educ 2.0 is found in **Table 2**: type of HTTP, page interarrival time, the properties of pages loaded, and the type of service.

The configurable parameters for video traffic (**Table 3**) are the values of packet arrival time (frame interarrival time), expressed by a constant value, and package size (frame size), which

Parameter	Value
Packets transmitted	575
Average packet per second	1.016
Average size of package	59.927 bytes
Average throughput	60.898 bytes/s

Table 1. Values DTV-EDUC 2.0.

Configuration parameter	Value
HTTP specification	HTTP 1.1
Page interarrival time (s)	Weibull (0.30419, 0.1139)
Page properties	Lognormal (4.2996, 0.25489)
Type of service	Best effort (0)

Table 2. Parameters for digital TV Application.

is a random variable with exponential distribution. The values assigned in these two variables generate a video application rate of 1.5 Mbps to each customer. The parameter type of service is also configured and represents that the priority will be given to the application on the network, which is the best effort type.

The configuration of the VoIP application is presented in **Table 4**. The times of silence and speech used to model the voice application parameters are represented by talk spurt and silence length. The parameters such as encoder scheme and voice frame per packet, characterize, respectively, the type of encoder used in the generation of voice traffic and the number of voice frames per packet during the simulation.

According to **Table 4**, the VoIP application uses the GSM encryption and generates a rate of approximately 20 kbps. The parameter type of service is also configured and represents the priority assigned to application on the network, which is best effort type.

Thus, applications have been developed and their characteristics were modeled using the parameters configurable by the simulator.

4.3. Simulation of a scenario

The development of the simulation tests required a tool that can simulate the performance of the network. Thus, an OPNET is the name of Network Simulator modeler was opted, which is widely used as a tool for modeling telecommunications networks, and their work environment allows creating a network from a library of templates, and set parameters not only for the environment, as well as for each object that is composed, and the impacts of its variations [37].

Configuration parameter	Value
Frame interarrival time (s)	Constant (0.1)
Frame size (bytes)	Exponential (15625)
Type of service	Best effort (0)

Table 3. Parameters for video application.

Configuration parameter	Value
Silence length (s)	Exponential (0.65)
Talk spurt length (s)	Exponential (0.352)
Encoder scheme	GSM (silence)
Voice frames per packet	1
Type of service	Best effort (0)

Table 4. Parameters for voice application.

Through this software, it was possible to observe the behavior of a network based on WiMAX, with the parameters defined in the previous section. **Figure 3** shows a scenario simulator that was set up containing 32 nodes, using the three streams defined above; a WiMAX antenna communicating with a backbone, which in turn communicates with the test server; box settings of the applications, the profiles, and WiMAX antenna.

Settings were made with parameters of real devices in order to make the simulation as realistic as possible, by applying these settings in the simulator. **Table 5** shows the main settings used in the simulation.

After analyzing the data input and configuration of the simulator, simulations were performed using a simulation time of 15 min to set up each scenario.

The tests were done thoroughly from the variation in the number of users on the network (until 40 users) and the change of seed of the simulation, which meant that for the same amount of users, different values were obtained. An extensive database was generated and consolidated, containing all the measured results of simulation experiments.

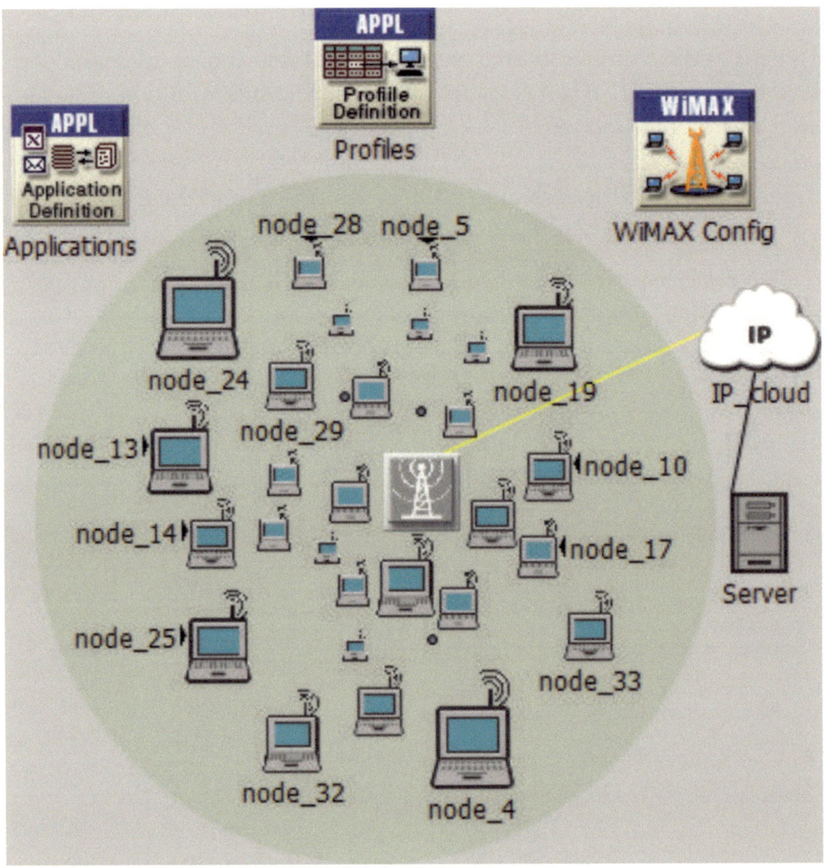

Figure 3. Scenario mounted on the OPNET simulator.

Parameter	Value
Frequency channel	5 MHz
Programming model	HATA
Antenna model	Ominidirecional
Gain transmission	1 dBm
Receive gain	1 dBm
Power transmission	0.125 dB
Length of frame	20 ms
Packet size	1024 bytes
Time of simulation	15 min

Table 5. WiMAX radio settings.

5. Generating the Bayesian network

After the organization of the database, computational intelligence model capable of extracting patterns was used. This model is Bayesian network that is used to assess the influence (weight) that each parameter has on the final result (selection of return channel).

BN is a model that codifies probabilistic relationships between variables that represent a certain domain. The BN is shaped by qualitative structure, expressing the dependencies among nodes, quantitative part (conditional probability tables of these nodes), quantifying these dependencies in probabilistic terms. To summarize, the cited components can give an efficient representation of the joint probability distribution of the set of variables for a given domain. More information can be obtained accessing Refs. [38–40].

BN was used given expertise of the group in BN area, exceptional analytical properties to expose domains, easy visualization and understanding of the relations among the variables, consisting on a crucial factor, and of great value for the representation and analysis of the domain (by the users).

For the Bayesian network, in order to establish correlations between the variables in the domain, it was necessary to define the attributes (metrics) considered for the analysis proposed in this chapter. These metrics were selected from the set of tests in the scenarios modeled in OPNET.

Thus, among the metrics provided by OPNET for analysis, seven were defined, which were used in the process of decision making. These metrics are shown in **Table 6**, as well as the description of their purpose.

From the definition of the metric (also called criteria) that would be used for decision making, a Bayesian network was generated using the search algorithm and scoring K2, widespread in the literature [41]. To this end, the application Bayesware Discoverer was employed. **Figure 4** shows the network generated from the tool, with seven nodes and their dependencies.

Metric	Description
Active connection	Total number of active TCP connections on the surrounding node.
Throughput	This statistic represents the average number of bits successfully received or transmitted by the receiver or transmitter channel per unit time, in bits per second.
Jitter	It is the value of delay variation, i.e., the difference between two delay times, measured in milliseconds.
Delay	Represents end-to-end delay of all the packets received by the WiMAX MACs of all WiMAX nodes in the network and forwarded to the higher layer.
Retransmissions	Number of TCP retransmissions on this node. Written when data is retransmitted from the TCP unacknowledged buffer.
Object response time	Specifies response time for each inlined object from the HTML page.
Data dropped	Higher layer data traffic dropped (in bits/s) by the WiMAX MAC due to data buffer overflow.

Table 6. Metrics used in the decision-making model.

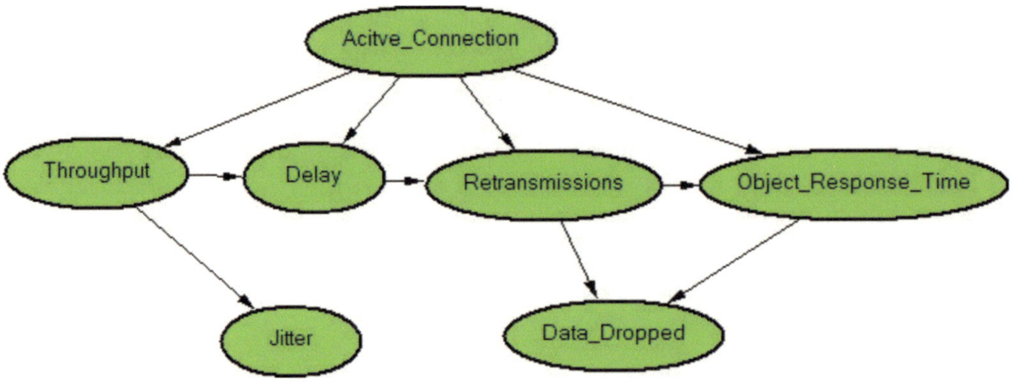

Figure 4. Bayesian network generated.

The goal of setting up the Bayesian network is to extract the weight that each criterion has measured in the simulation environment. Thus, a weight vector was generated to the application of the TOPSIS method for decision making, considering the Probability distribution shown in **Figure 5**.

We set up the conditional entropy (Eq. (1)) as a measure of the uncertainty that obtains the value of Y is known as X. If the value of $(X, Y) \sim p\,(x, y)$, then the conditional entropy $H\,(Y|X)$.

$$H(Y|X) = \sum_{x \in X} p(x) H(Y|X = x) \tag{1}$$

Guiding on the theory proposed for Bayesian networks, we could verify the impact that alterations between the states of the variable X cause on the states of the variable Y. That means, when we infer the state $Xi = 1$, for example, we determine the impact that the first X state is causing on the states of the variable Y. Then, we were able to verify the impact that each X

http://dx.doi.org/10.5772/intechopen.69615

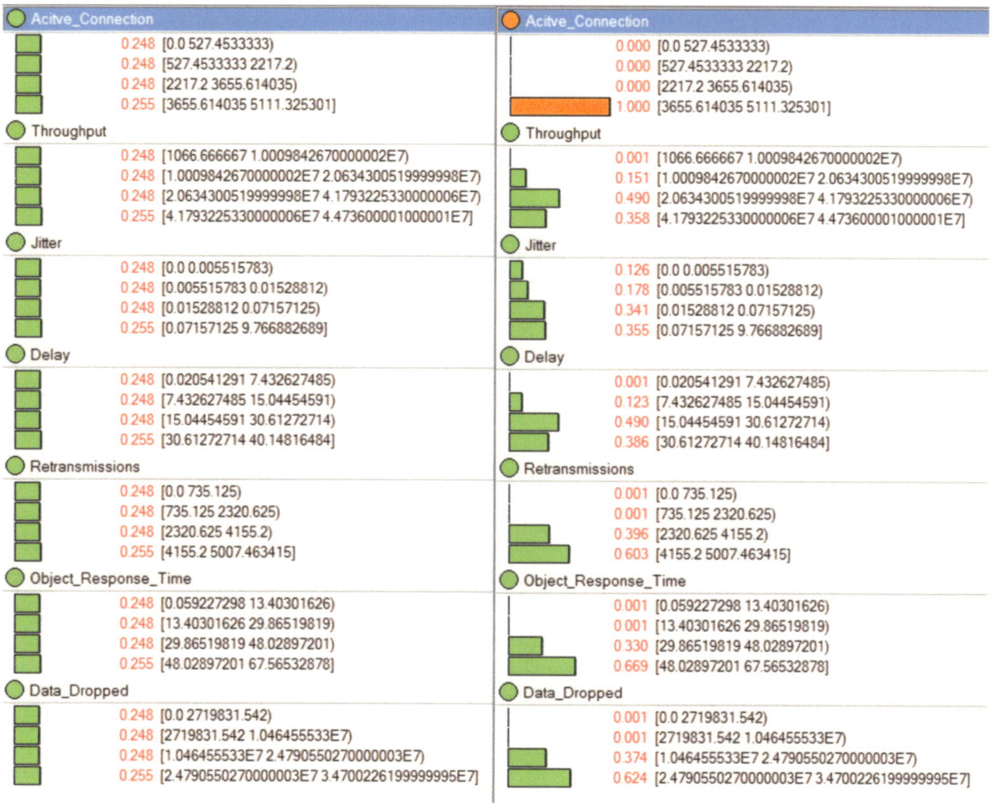

Figure 5. Probability distribution.

state was influencing on *Y*; in this case, the quantity of inference done in all states of the base-variables of the three defined factors was affecting the states of the other variable, which we aim to determine the weight. This influence from each state on the variable *X* over *Y* is added together, obtaining a vector of probability *V*p.

$V\text{p} = [0.24\ 0.27\ 0.27\ 0.08\ 0.07\ 0.07]$

Weight values for each criterion obtained from the Bayesian network express the influence that certain criteria have about setting the scene.

Thus, by extrapolating the fitted model and assuming that a service provider has more than one choice of access technology for a given scenario, the purpose of this chapter is to define what technology should be used.

6. Tests to evaluate the first miles

From the weights defined, real test scenarios and experiments were performed to test the proposed strategies.

In order to perform measurements in real scenarios, three access technologies were used such as PLC, WiMAX, and ADSL. The choice of these different technologies is based on the availability of resources for testing and the focus of these tests on heterogeneous networks, since the metrics analyzed should provide different values due to each technology's peculiarities.

WiMAX networks, for example, suffer interference caused by external factors such as distance between antennas and similar frequencies. PLC networks, which use electricity to transfer data, suffer interference caused by devices that operate in frequency bands similar to those used for data transmission. ADSL technology uses fixed telephony lines for data transmission and is characterized by impulsive and background noises.

Thus, scenarios were set to test the different types of technologies, as illustrated in **Figure 1**, based on four layers already defined. Then, a java applet to obtain the results of the criteria established was employed.

Based on the sampling theory, the tests performed were repeated over 50 times, to obtain an acceptable average for comparison. The average results are shown in **Table 7**.

The values shown in **Table 7** show the average of the results obtained from 1 to 40 users. These numbers represent measurements from real-world scenarios at any given time and were used in the decision-making process presented in this chapter.

From these values, a decision-making framework using TOPSIS was implemented to calculate decision making based on weights previously obtained.

7. Heuristics for decision making

After the evaluation on real scenarios of the access technologies (PLC, WiMAX and ADSL), a decision of which technology to be used follows. For the decision making, TOPSIS method is

	PLC	**WiMAX**	**ADSL**
Number of active connections	1.000	2.227	3.000
Average jitter (ms)	4.8	6.7	3.1
Average delay (ms)	16.6	21	13.5
Average throughput (kbps)	716	1436.6	6912.5
Object response time (s)	31.6	25.8	21.9
Number of data dropped	2.500	1.800	1.100
Number of retransmissions	3.000	3.700	2.200

Table 7. Results with different technologies.

Country	Throughput	Jitter	Delay	Retransmissions	Object_response_time	Data_dropped	Prioritaet
ADSL	0,186154494	0,09505228146	0,1215804061	0,03354359188208	0,0331092242482394	0,02353958684215	0,9999999
WiMAX	0,138188686	0,20543557607	0,1891250762	0,05641422271077	0,0390053874705286	0,03851932392352	0,3567272
PLC	0,062051498	0,14717772614	0,1494988697	0,04574126165738	0,0477740404677792	0,05349906100490	0,3341741
Weight	0,24	0,27	0,27	0,08	0,07	0,07	(nulo)
max/mi	1	0	0	0	0	0	(nulo)

Figure 6. Results with different technologies.

applied on the results measured from the network (**Table 7**), based on the vector *Vp*, which is the weight for each metric evaluated.

Using an applet, the results were compared with other applications available in the market to see the degree of certainty, all of which were proved satisfactorily.

Figure 6 shows the relative closeness to the ideal solution, ranking the alternatives in increasing order of selection.

In this case, from the use of the results of real scenarios, the best choice to service provider is the ADSL technology as it presented the best performance compared to other technologies.

If for some reason (financial, political, etc.), ADSL technology cannot be used, the WiMAX network would be selected and, as a last alternative, the PLC technology. If in case, a new evaluation is made on the networks, or another service is available with different weights, a new score table must be generated.

8. Conclusion

The papers, to serve as a basis for this chapter, surveyed for showed that several studies are being conducted in areas covered: access technologies, service provider, Digital TV, and decision support.

After analyzing the papers, gaps were found that need attention, among which are the lack of studies using a heuristic, based on multicriteria analysis, using data collected; testing implementations on real devices; implementation of these heuristic in open platforms; setting up a consolidated database from simulation scenarios; using TOPSIS from a weight vector based on simulation tests, not experts; and comparison of different technologies that are already consolidated in the market.

Thus, this chapter presents a novel strategy that considers the use of real test scenarios, drawing a comparison between more than one access technologies such as PLC, WiMAX, and ADSL. This comparison is performed by a heuristic decision making, based on the Bayesian networks and TOPSIS, which measures the best choice of the access technology.

Access providers can plan for optimizing interactive services for digital TV, using a heuristic that considers seven network performance measures active connection, jitter, delay, throughput, object response time, data dropped, and retransmissions.

As future studies, new tests will be conducted with other access technologies, for confirming the results obtained in these experiments. In addition, new techniques will be adopted to optimize the system, such as genetic algorithms and Markov decision process. Furthermore, the proposed criteria will be improved to obtain other measures for network performance.

Author details

Marcos César da Rocha Seruffo[1]*, Ádamo Lima de Santana[1], Carlos Renato Lisboa Francês[1] and Nandamudi Lankalapalli Vijaykumar[2]

*Address all correspondence to: marcos.seruffo@gmail.com

1 Federal University of Pará, Belém, Pará, Brazil

2 National Institute for Space Research (INPE), São José dos Campos, São Paulo, Brazil

References

[1] Brazilian Institute of Geography and Statistics (IBGE). National Survey by Household Sample [Internet]. 2009. Available from: <http://www.ibge.gov.br/home/estatistica/populacao/trabalhoerendimento/pnad2009/default.shtm> [Accessed: January 31 2017]

[2] Montez C, Becker V. Interactive Digital TV: Concepts, Challenges and Prospects for Brazil. UFSC Publishing company, Second Edition; 2005

[3] Prado GM, Zorzo SD. Interactive service provider architecture for interactive digital television systems. In: 2010 International Conference on Computer Information Systems and Industrial Management Applications (CISIM); 2010

[4] Costanzo BP, Neto JA. Analysis of the Brazilian digital TV system (BDTVS) and signal-converting devices. In: Portland International Center for Management of Engineering and Technology (PICMET). Annals; 2007. pp. 1830-1838

[5] Xiao Y, et al. Internet protocol television (IPTV): The killer application for the next-generation internet. IEEE Communications Magazine. 2007;**45**(11):126-134

[6] Dutta-roy A. Bring home the internet. Journal IEEE Spectrum. 2012;**39**(12):32-38

[7] Budri AK, et al. WiMAX simulation models for return channel in digital television systems. In: International Telecommunications Symposium. Annals; Fortaleza. Vol. 3; 2006. pp. 688-693

[8] Polo EI, et al. PLC as a return channel for interactive digital TV. In: International Conference on Communications and Networking in China. Annals; Shangai, China; 2007. pp. 1-5

[9] Campista MEM, et al. The ad hoc return channel: A low-cost solution for Brazilian interactive digital TV. IEEE Communications Magazine. 2007;**45**(1):136-143

[10] Nasser N. A Theoretical approach for service provider decision in heterogeneous wireless networks. In: IEEE Communications Society Subject Matter Experts for Publication in the IEEE CCNC 2016 Proceedings; 2016

[11] Hideyuki K, et al. Combined adaptive congestion control method for communication-broadcasting integrated services. In: Global Telecommunications Conference. Annals; 2006. p. 1

[12] Hideyuki K, et al. Access control method based on sample monitoring for volatile traffic in interactive TV services. In: Global Telecommunications Conference. Annals; 2008. pp. 16

[13] Habiba U, Asghar S. A survey on multi-criteria decision making approaches. In: International Conference on Emerging Technologies ICET 2009; 2009. Pp. 321-325

[14] Levin M. Selection of user´s connection in last-mile problem. IEEE Transaction on System, Man, and Cybernetics—Part a: Systems and Humans. 2011;**41**(2):370-374

[15] Kabat MR, Patel MK, Tripathy CR. A heuristic algorithm for core selection in multicast routing. Journal of Computer Science and Technology. 2011;**26**(6):954=961

[16] Charilas DE, et al. Application of fuzzy AHP and ELECTRE to network selection. Mobile Lightweight Wireless Systems. Lecture Notes of the Institute for Computer Sciences Social Informatics and Telecommunications Engineering. 2009;**13**:63-73

[17] Sgora A, et al. An access network selection algorithm for heterogeneous wireless environments. In: IEEE Symposium on Computers and Communications (ISCC), 2010; 2010

[18] Sgora A, et al. Network selection in a WiMAX-WiFi environment. Journal of Pervasive and Mobile Computing. 2010;**7**(5):584-594

[19] Chen Y. Fuzzy AHP-based method for project risk assessment. In: Conference on Fuzzy Systems and Knowledge Discovery (FSDK); 2010; Yantai, Shandong. Annals; 2010. pp. 1249=1253

[20] Yan G, et al. The design and application of a generic AHP evaluation system. In: 4th International Conference on Wireless Communications, Networking and Mobile Computing (WICOM); 2008; Donghua Univ., Shanghai. Annals; 2008. p. 1

[21] Chunhao L, et al. An improved ranking approach to AHP alternatives based on variable weights. In: 7th World Congress on Intelligent Control and Automation (WCICA); 2008. Annals. Jilin Univ., Changchun; 2008. pp. 8255-8260

[22] Zhe Fu, Delcroix V. Bayesian network based on the method of AHP for making decision. In: Information Technology and Artificial Intelligence Conference (ITAIC), 2011 6th IEEE Joint International; 2011

[23] Sun Xuan. A Novel Kind of Decision of Weight of Multi-attribute Decision-Making Model Based on Bayesian Networks. In: International Seminar on Business and Information Management (ISBIM 08); 2008

[24] Xuan S, Qinzhou N, Hefei X. A Bayesian method for decision of weight for MADM model with interval data. In: International Conference on Advanced Computer Control (ICACC 09); 2009

[25] Supraja S, Kousalya P. A comparative study by AHP and TOPSIS for the selection of all round excellence award. In: International Conference on Electrical, Electronics, and Optimization Techniques (ICEEOT); 2016

[26] Nag K, Helal M. A Fuzzy TOPSIS approach in multi-criteria decision making for supplier selection in a pharmaceutical distributor. In: International Conference on Industrial Engineering and Engineering Management (IEEM); 2016; IEEE; 2016

[27] Kaur S, Sehra SK, Sehra SS. A framework for software quality model selection using TOPSIS. In: IEEE International Conference on Recent Trends in Electronics, Information & Communication Technology (RTEICT); 2017

[28] Larasati AA, Setyaningrum AH, Wardhani LK. Development decision support system of choosing medicine using TOPSIS method (Case Study: RSIA Tiara). In: 6th International Conference on Information and Communication Technology for The Muslim World (ICT4M); 2016

[29] Sari WP, Cahyaningsih E, Sensuse DI, Noprisson H. The welfare classification of Indonesian national civil servant using TOPSIS and k-Nearest Neighbour (KNN). In: 2016 IEEE Student Conference on Research and Development (SCOReD); 2016

[30] Loganathan J, Latchoumi TP, Janakiraman S, Parthiban L. A novel multi-criteria channel decision in co-operative cognitive radio network using E-TOPSIS. In: International Conference on Informatics and Analytics (ICIA); 2016

[31] Costa CAB. Absolute and relative evaluation problematiques: The concept of neutral level and the MCDA robot technique. In: Proceedings of the International Multicriteria Decision Making Workshop; 1991; Lieblice, Março. Annals; 1991. pp. 7-15

[32] Salehi M, Moghaddam TR. Project selection by using a Fuzzy topsis technique. World Academy of Science, Engineering and Technology. 2008;**2**(4):375-380

[33] Bankmaz B, Bojkovic Z, Bakmaz M. Network selection algorithm for heterogeneous wireless environment. In: XXVII Annual IEEE International Symposium on Personal, Indoor and Mobile Radio Communications (PICK) 2007;2007

[34] Lo C, et al. Service selection based on fuzzy Topsis method. In: IEEE 24th International Conference on Advanced Information Networking and Applications Workshops (WAYNE), 2010; 2010

[35] Seruffo MCR, Monteiro FP, Silva CN, Jacob Junior AFL, Cardoso DL, Francês CRLC. DTV-EDUC 2.0: A case study of interactive educational application for Digital TV. In: 20th International Symposium on Digital Television; 2011

[36] Castro MC. Proposals for implementing quality of service in MPLS VPN architecture using formal specification language SDL object-oriented and performance analysis using OPNET simulator [thesis]. Dissertation submitted to the Faculty of Electrical Engineering and Computer Sciences; 2004

[37] OPNET Modeler. Available from http://www.opnet.com

[38] Chen Z. Data Mining and Uncertain Reasoning—An Integrated Approach. John Wiley Professional; 2001

[39] Korb KB, Nicholson. Bayesian Artificial Intelligence. CRC Press Publishing company, Second Edition; 2003

[40] Pearl J. Probabilistic Reasoning in Intelligent System. Morgan Kaufmann Publishing company; 1988

[41] Chen XW, Anantha G, Lin X. Improving bayesian network structure learning with mutual information-based node ordering in the K2 algorithm. In: IEEE Transactions on Knowledge and Data Engineering; 2008;**20**(5):628-640